COPING
WITH
INFERTILITY

COPING
WITH
INFERTILITY

Judith A. Stigger

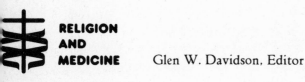

RELIGION AND MEDICINE

Glen W. Davidson, Editor

AUGSBURG Publishing House • Minneapolis

COPING WITH INFERTILITY

Copyright © 1983 Augsburg Publishing House

Library of Congress Catalog Card No. 82-072649
International Standard Book No. 0-8066-1956-2

Scripture quotations unless otherwise noted are from the Revised Standard
Version of the Bible, copyright 1946, 1952, and 1971 by the Division
of Christian Education of the National Council of Churches.

Scripture quotations marked GNB are from the Good News Bible (Today's
English Version) © 1976 American Bible Society

MANUFACTURED IN THE UNITED STATES OF AMERICA

IN APPRECIATION

To those infertile persons who shared unstintingly of painful
memories and the wisdom gleaned from experience;

To family and friends who advised, encouraged and supported me as I wrote this book;

To Doctors Julian Archie, Shahid Ekbal and Donald
Woznica for technical assistance on medical issues;

To Judy and George Fitchett who got me started writing;

To Bernice Klosterman (my mother), Mary Rinder, and
Sherry Lombardo who cared for my children (adopted);

To my husband, Bob.

IN HOPE

That those who now contend with the pain of infertility
might suffer less.

The names of the infertile persons who contributed to this
book have been changed to protect their privacy.

Contents

Foreword

Infertility affects an estimated 12% of the nation's couples of childbearing age. They number approximately 9 million, even more when couples plagued by miscarriages are added. To these millions, attempts at pregnancy require the contrivance of medical intervention which turn sexual privacy into a laboratory affair. Basal Temperature Graphs dictate the moments of romance. Submission to repeated pelvic examinations and collection of semen specimens become as inevitable as receipt of the monthly bills.

For centuries, and in some countries still, women unable to bear children were cast out of the family. Men unable to sire offspring were ostracized. Most childless couples report that even in this enlightened age they find very little understanding and receive a great deal of thoughtless advice. As a result, they tend to isolate themselves, believing that they alone face the crisis of infertility. Their feelings of loss—loss of well-being, loss of spontaneous sharing—become an obsession. Yet, with whom can they share their emotions? Their feelings of guilt, depression, and conflict place even greater stress on the problems they face in their marriages, their jobs, and their social relationships.

Infertility research and treatment are leading to major medical breakthroughs. Often, however, these are exaggerated in the public media and generalized to apply to conditions beyond the researcher's intentions. This, coupled with our society's religious devotion to medical progress, allows many infertile couples to build false hopes and expectations for themselves. Their dreams for the future become despair. Their zest for living turns into self-pity and rage. Even for those couples fortunate to become pregnant, they are often left emotionally and spiritually scarred by the crisis.

Like the other books in Augsburg's RELIGION AND MEDICINE SERIES, *Coping with Infertility* addresses one of life's problems with medically competent information and theological sensitivity. The purpose of the book is not to instruct readers on how to achieve pregnancy, but rather to assist those who wrestle with infertility to resolve their emotional and spiritual crises. It is written as much for the couples who succeed in pregnancy as for those who do not.

Judith A. Stigger lives with her lawyer husband and two adopted children in Oak Park, Illinois. She writes with a conviction that is based on experience. In addition, Judith brings to her writing the insights and skills of a mental-health specialist. She graduated from Macalester College in 1971, served a year in Afghanistan with the Peace Corps, and received her masters degree from the University of Chicago's School of Social Service Administration in 1975. She is a member of the Academy of Certified Social Workers and is active in her local church.

Glen W. Davidson, Ph.D.
Professor and Chairman
Department of Medical Humanities
Southern Illinois University
School of Medicine

Who Should Read
this Book and Why

Infertile or Possibly Infertile Persons

This book is for couples who are or who fear they might be infertile. The experience of infertility can be frighteningly isolating. Suddenly the whole world appears to be pregnant: one passes scores of conspicuously pregnant people every day without seeing a single conspicuously infertile person. A fear begins to grow that this trauma of infertility is unique, that no one else is capable of comprehending or appreciating the emotional pain.

Yet in the United States, at least 12 percent of all marriages are estimated to be involuntarily barren. Approximately half of these couples eventually conceive, many only following medical intervention. Half remain barren. Another 15 percent of couples conceive, but miscarry or suffer stillbirths. (Miscarriage is beyond the scope of this book. See p. 109 for suggested reading concerning miscarriage.) Still others bear a first child, but then are unable to conceive a second. These couples too know the sorrow and frustration of not having a desired baby.

Part of the infertile couple's sense of isolation arises out of their perception that infertility is an invisible or concealable problem. This perception is not always accurate. When I mentioned to friends that I was writing this book, almost all could identify one or more couples whom I might interview. In several instances the infertile couple did not realize that others suspected the situation. When approached, they were startled, even chagrined, but grateful that a friend cared enough to discern and acknowledge their plight.

As couples realize they are not alone, they may feel less isolated or abnormal. As they learn that others subjected to the same trauma have found a predictable pattern within the seeming chaos of feelings, they may realize that their emotions are not random or crazy and that others have shared their situation. Infertile couples suffer enough without feelings of isolation compounding their misery.

Family and Friends

This book is for the family and friends of infertile couples. Infertility is a condition which a couple may find great difficulty discussing or mentioning even to the closest family and friends, so an infertile couple often suffers in silence. Others possibly sense that something is amiss; the strain or depression may be evident, although the cause may not. One may be reasonably certain that a couple is trying to have a child, but wonder whether or how to broach the subject.

I have a friend who gave birth to a severely retarded child. With the birth announcement she included a letter explaining what had happened and how she hoped others would react. She requested that family and friends acknowledge the baby, but not pretend that he was normal. She hoped this letter would help those who "did not know what to say" to risk saying something, and help those who were willing to respond to choose words of comfort more skillfully.

Infertility is not as concrete and identifiable a sadness as the birth of a profoundly retarded child. But the pain is real. It is vital that family and friends say something to acknowledge the significance of their loved one's distress. To ignore the issue implies that infertility is not important enough or too unpleasant to discuss. The former diminishes the validity and magnitude of the suffering; the latter distances or isolates. Since most family and friends do not intend these results, they should invite discussion.

How one acknowledges another's infertility, or possible infertility, is of no less importance. Every person I interviewed recalled instances of feeling comforted by compassionate words and other instances of feeling mocked by careless platitudes. As family and friends better understand the infertile person's experience and needs, they can more sensitively come to the aid of their loved ones. This book attempts to assist in that most difficult art of caring.

Counselors and Clergy

This book is for counselors and clergy. I hope to offer information in three areas. First, I wish to give those in the helping professions insight into the scope and seriousness of the problem. Before my infertility, I had no idea that one in eight couples of childbearing age are infertile, nor did I understand how shattering an experience infertility can be. The lack of literature on this subject results, in part, because social workers, psychiatrists, and hospital chaplains—the authors of books on the emotional implications of other medical problems—rarely are called on to counsel the infertile patient. The diagnosis and treatment of infertility does not require an extensive hospital stay.

Second, I wish to encourage counselors to educate themselves concerning infertility. Prior to my own experience, I knew no theory specifically related to the emotional stages of infertility. These stages are not especially difficult to discern. Once I suggested the stages to them, the infertile people with whom I talked in researching this book accurately located themselves. Most were interested to see how their situation deviated from my "textbook model." Many were relieved by the assurance that their reactions to infertility were typical.

Third, I wish to encourage counselors to offer services for infertile couples and their families. Little counseling is available. Resolve, a self-help group that works in consultation with physicians and professional counselors, is beginning to offer its services nationwide. Otherwise, in the Chicago area, for instance, I know of only one hospital with a social worker attached to its outpatient infertility clinic. She is there because of the insistence of an influential former patient. Yet even patients at this hospital are not always informed that counseling is available. If counseling were offered—if, for instance, a book on infertility were visible on a social worker's shelves or a hospital chaplain made infertility specialists associated with the hospital aware of the services a chaplain can offer—more infertile people might avail themselves of this help.

From a counselor's standpoint, infertility can be a rewarding area in which to work. Clients are usually basically healthy and react positively to both empathy and instruction; stages move quickly; and the resolution of feelings is often dramatic and gratifying. Many people need help with infertility problems and too few counselors offer such help.

Physicians and Medical Staff Who Treat Infertility

This book is for physicians and other medical personnel who treat infertile couples. A doctor influences the attempts of most infertile couples to cope emotionally. All the people I interviewed volunteered comments on their physician's sensitivity to emotional issues. Two praised their doctors; the rest criticized theirs harshly. No one seemed neutral on this topic.

Physicians necessarily influence couples for at least two reasons. A physician typically meets with an infertile couple frequently over an extended period of time, perhaps several years. During this time, the physician is intimately involved in the couple's every attempt to conceive: monitoring ovulation, counting sperm, administering tests and interpreting results, and recording each month's disappointment. With such frequent and intimate involvement in the quest for a baby, the doctor's attitude and actions influence the couple's perceptions of themselves and of their infertility.

Second, having never before been diagnosed concerning their infertility, the couple has few guidelines against which to evaluate their medical prognosis or their emotional adjustment. They look to their physician for information about all aspects of infertility and for expertise in treatment. Their lack of experience with infertility work-ups, and their dependence upon the doctor to supply a cure, can make the couple reluctant to question the diagnosis or advice of their "expert," even when they suspect that the physician may have missed something. "He is the doctor; he must know what he is doing." This reluctance may continue, even when they recognize that a particular action or attitude is hurting them emotionally, because couples fear that an expression of their feelings might impede the doctor's progress toward that medical cure for which they so desperately long.

Reluctance in offering feedback to the doctor, especially when paired with the doctor's failure to solicit it, allows a physician to exercise a considerable influence on the patients' emotional health yet be oblivious to that influence.

Having chosen to treat infertile couples and not being able to abdicate involvement in the couple's emotional well-being, physicians should educate themselves concerning the emotional components of infertility. Awareness of the patients' emotions and possible responses to these emotions may allow a doctor to avoid doing emotional damage, while supporting mental health and eliciting more accurate medical information. With an understanding of the emotional stages of infertility, a doctor may recognize points in the couple's adjustment to infertility at which particular support is appropriate. Using this same understanding of the normal progression of feelings during infertility, a doctor may more easily identify patient couples who are suffering unusual distress and are in need of counseling beyond the scope of the physician's expertise.

1

Defining Infertility

Infertility may be defined as the inability to achieve pregnancy within a stipulated period of time.[1] The "stipulated period of time" varies among different cultures. In Afghanistan, a Middle-eastern Moslem country, a man may divorce his wife without social stigma if she does not conceive within two years of their marriage. In the United States, until recently, an infertility investigation before three years of barrenness was considered medically premature.[2]

Today, in the United States, the "stipulated period" is usually one year. At least two factors have prompted the shorter waiting time. First, the medical profession has begun to appreciate that infertility causes a couple psychological stress. Sometimes a simple explanation can reduce the couple's fear and uncertainty, which, if left unattended, might later cause major trauma. If a simple explanation is not possible, the inception of a search for the cause of their infertility still serves to validate the couple's concerns about their problem and directs their attempts toward solving it. While the search does not eliminate the couple's emotional distress, it does involve them in activity aimed at solving their problem: it offers purposefulness and hope.

Second, individuals are choosing to marry later, and many couples are delaying their first pregnancy until their thirties. A 20-year-old woman who has been trying unsuccessfully for one year to conceive causes less medical concern than a 35-year-old woman in the same circumstances. At thirty-five years of age a woman can ill afford to wait two more years before beginning medical exploration of the couple's infertility.

But even a one-year "stipulated period" is arbitrary when human emotions are involved. Infertility has a significant emotional component in addition to the medical component. An adequate definition of infertility must include this emotional component. For the purpose of this book a couple will be considered emotionally infertile at the point *when they decide that too much time has passed without conception.* For instance, when the question arises, "Should we try one more month, or should I call a doctor?" when one prays for conception during intercourse, or when either partner begins to fear that getting pregnant might not be as automatic as had been assumed, that couple is "infertile."

Given this definition, the "stipulated period" for any couple is unique to that couple. I have a South American friend whose husband took her to a physician one month after their marriage; he was concerned because she was not yet pregnant. This is an example of a situation in which a simple explanation by a doctor relieved a couple's distress.

I became concerned after about six months. The doctor I consulted initially taught me to use a Basal Temperature Graph (see Chapter 4), patted my hand, and told me my concern was premature, which only fueled my anxiety because then I worried about being worried. Three months later a visit to another physician initiated our infertility work-up.

Jean and Fred had waited three years before seeking medical advice. They had felt ready for a child if one came, but not in any hurry. Only after they became concerned that they might be incapable of ever bearing a child did they consult their doctor.

Anna and Bill already had one child. After six months of trying to have a second, Anna noticed that the pregnancy seemed long in coming, but she did not worry since she "knew" she was fertile. Only after a year had passed did she admit concern to Bill, and another four months passed before they contacted their physician.

This discussion assumes that consciousness of infertility creeps up on a couple. While this is the more common advent of the problem, occasionally infertility confronts a couple abruptly. For example, June suffered a stillbirth accompanied by severe medical complications. She and her husband were faced with probable infertility suddenly.

Regardless of how gradually or abruptly infertility comes, it initiates a change in self-image that must be absorbed and adjusted to. This book explores that adjustment period. A model is offered of the progression of events and stages which takes place as previous assumptions of fertility are shed, permitting reconciliation of the accumulating evidence of infertility. The model does not consist of a series of tidy stages, but rather a process of transition. The order of events and emotions within stages may be altered by circumstances, such as the abrupt onset of infertility, but the integrity of the stages remains.

2

Emotional Stages of Infertility

The Assumption of Fertility

I always assumed I was fertile. Most people do. The assumption begins to develop during early childhood. A child forms much of his or her self-image by identifying with parents—and they have children. Most other significant adults, for example, parents of playmates and grandparents, also have children. To a small child, all adults are mommies and daddies, or if gray-haired, grandmas or grandpas. Children may not understand other grown-up roles such as an accountant or secretary, but they have some concept of what it is to be a parent.

Information from books and television supports the universality of the parent role (and implicitly of fertility). To quote a story aimed at preschoolers:

FATHER: "I'm a father.
          I'm a he.
          A *father's* something
          you could be."

MOTHER: "I'm a mother.
          I'm a she.

A *mother's* something
you could be."

KIDS: "Those are things that we could be
just because we're he and she."[1]

Teenagers understand that many choices are involved in the transition from childhood to adulthood, and concern themselves with those choices which seem more urgent, for example, future education, career, and marriage partner. The option to have children is assumed to be available to everyone; the decision concerning children can be made later. Warnings by parents not to become pregnant or get a girl pregnant, and the incidence of pregnancies among acquaintances, bolster the assumption. Those teenagers having difficulty finding adult roles, or feeling insecure in relationships with the opposite sex, may choose to (or "accidentally") become pregnant or father a child to prove that they are growing up.

Having made decisions about career and spouse, adults consider becoming parents. That the option to bear children exists is a foregone conclusion. "We had planned our life so that schooling and training came first, and then children. We fully believed that the first shot at conception would result in pregnancy. We simply could not believe it when we failed to conceive after the first two months of trying."[2]

Only if one has known adults who were unable to bear children does one grow up appreciating that children are not automatic. This was the case with Jay. His aunt and uncle were involuntarily childless. They lived next door and helped raise him and his several brothers. When Jay recognized that he and his wife were infertile, he was very unhappy, but not surprised. "I always knew infertility could happen." Because he was already aware of the existence of the condition, he could adjust to the problem more quickly.

When I was 26, we decided to exercise our option to have children. Nothing happened. Not until I was confronted with possible infertility did I realize just how concrete was my assumption and my image of the child I would bear. Without intentionally considering it, I had created an "assumption child." She or he would have brown hair, brown eyes (crossed unfortunately), a bright mind, and impeccable prenatal care. When this child did not happen as planned, I was dumbfounded.

The possibility of infertility threatens the role of parent and the existence of that "assumption child." One reacts by bolstering the assumption of fertility with a three-tiered defense system.

Defending the Assumption

The first level of defense is to deny that a problem exists. "Surely next month we'll get pregnant." "There's no problem. I'm just overanxious." Such denial protects the hope that the assumptions need no altering and serves to ward off the confusion felt when an assumption is challenged.

Initial denial is healthy in that it softens the jolt of possible infertility. Initial denial is also realistic, since several months often pass before conception in fertile couples. (Assuming good health and intercourse at least twice a week, 50% of couples conceive within six months and another 30% within a year.)

But while initial denial of possible infertility is useful, prolonged denial is not. Prolonged denial may take such forms as a declaration that such matters are "in God's hands," or up to Mother Nature, or that "on second thought, we did not really want children." The longer a problem is denied, without resolution, the less realistic the denial becomes and the more emotional effort the denial demands. Protracted denial blocks healthy coping and resolution and prevents the seeking of appropriate medical help.

Initial denial ends with the acknowledgment that an infertility problem may exist. This acknowledgment usually leads to a quest for medical services. Even then, one may retreat occasionally to denial for a respite from the emotional strain of infertility. "Surely God is just testing me," may be the first reaction to the trauma of a particularly painful visit to the doctor. For a few minutes, one allows oneself to believe.

The second line of defense is to acknowledge that a fertility problem exists, but deny responsibility for it. Responsibility may be avoided by blaming another for the problem. A spouse is vulnerable because he or she is available (or unavailable) ; if medically culpable, he or she is all the more likely a target. Or responsibility is escaped by foisting on someone else the task of correcting infertility. If the spouse is to blame, then she or he should be obligated to find a cure or at least to shoulder the brunt of the emotional distress. An alternative target is the doctor. Being the expert, the doctor should take responsibility for dealing with the infertility.

Another way to disown a problem is to declare it unfair or beyond one's capabilities. Like a young child giving a problem back to a parent, "It's too hard for me; you do it," one hands responsibility for the cure to whomever or whatever one believes to be in control. "I didn't do anything to deserve this. It's unfair. I wash my hands of the whole thing." "God, you did this damage. You repair it."

Jo Ann was unable to conceive. After several years of trying, she adamantly denied any problem. Such matters were up to God, who would act in his infinite wisdom. Believing thus, she refused to seek medical help.

Meanwhile, babies became an obsession with her. She kept in her purse a carefully chosen list of over 50 possible names, just in case God chose to bless her. Suppressing all anger and doubt exhausted her emotionally, and she mired down at this point. She became more and more detached from the reality of her situation.

After six years, she did give birth. By then, containing those unresolved feelings had destroyed her ability to respond to new events in her life. She could not cope with the demands

oneself as not worthy or attempts to decipher a message from
God; acceptance that God has chosen not to intervene; or
abandonment of faith. The second and third alternatives
eliminate hope for a cure by supernatural means.

The realization that the experts have failed marks the
destruction of the third and final line of defense. Infertility
cannot be denied, or avoided, and may not be solvable. The
child of one's assumptions is dying. How can anything wanted
so desperately fail to happen!

Relinquishing the Assumption

Lea told me of her moment of recognition. She had a
dream. Babies floated in front of her—babies with faces like
those of her and her husband's baby pictures. When she
reached out to hold one, it would flit out of range and fade
away. She awoke crying hysterically. But as she sobbed, she
realized why she had been so depressed the last three months.
These were the babies she would never have. She was grieving
for them. Realizing that she was mourning her "assumption
children" did not eliminate her pain. But at least, now, she
understood; for that she felt relief. Others may never grasp
intellectually what is happening to them emotionally. They
suffer through this stage, wondering if their depression will
ever end.

A part of the self has been lost—the fertile, potential
parent. Confidence in one's sexual identity and worth is
shaken, and all the resources of emotional energy must be
summoned to avert disintegration of the remainder of that
depleted self-image. Because all the emotional energy is tied
into maintaining what is left of self, no energy is available
for anything else. Couples I talked to reported feeling drained,
apathetic, and lifeless. Just maintaining daily functioning is
a chore. Nothing is done spontaneously, because spontaneity
requires an output of energy. Life contains little joy. I worried
that I did not laugh any more.

One approach for coping is to try to deny the grief and accompanying depression, perhaps by staying busy and keeping the mind focused on other concerns. Men seem to use this coping mechanism more effectively than women I talked to. As Bill said, "my concern was for my wife. She wanted a child so badly. I really did not care. I enjoyed our life-style and my work. I did not have much time to think about kids. It was a lot harder on her." A similar report came from Lian. "His disappointment is mitigated by involvement in a job he likes and other interests. I have not found a satisfactory alternative."[8] Keeping busy at work which provides satisfaction offers some distraction from the awareness of infertility.

In spite of these efforts to control it, grief impinges. Reminders that one has no control over fertility are ever-present; a coworker becomes pregnant or a neighbor's child runs past the window. Testing also keeps the problem in the forefront. A Basal Temperature Chart requires starting each day by sticking a thermometer in one's mouth, lest one forget one has a problem. Sex is regulated by the doctor rather than desire. As my husband said, "I felt like a milkman. And what was worse, I was not even sure I was delivering enough milk." Every period brings the frustration of failure. My husband's outstanding memory is of my rushing from the bathroom, sobbing, because my period had started—again. He would hold me in his arms, and I would cry myself numb. The numbness let me go to work and function.

Infertile couples often grieve alone. When a person loses a living relative, other family and friends know; they gather to console and support. Talking of the loss and receiving expressions of caring from others helps the person absorb and accept the event. The opportunity to "talk it out" is an aid to healing. In contrast, no one but the spouse and physician may be aware of the loss of an "assumption child." If the infertile person wants the support of others, she or he must usually seek that support, explaining the circumstances and the need for caring. To do this requires an awareness of what is happening and sufficient resolution to the change in self-image to expose this "defect." Until that resolution occurs, and until the embarrassment most infertile people feel can be overcome, the only outlet and source of support may be a spouse. "By nature reticent, I found it difficult to reach out to family or friends, to admit to outsiders that I had a problem. . . . I leaned heavily on my husband, so heavily that my dependence dragged him down."[9] One feels guilt for placing this extra burden on a spouse who is already in pain.

Isolation stresses marriage. Both spouses are depleted at the time each needs extra confirmation of worth from the other. "The threat of divorce was a direct result of the infertility and a confirmation of my failure as a woman."[10] Feelings of unworthiness, for example, at having deprived one's spouse of the chance to procreate may cause one to refuse what support the spouse is able to offer.

Friendships, another possible source of support, are also strained. Not having experienced infertility, friends may not realize its impact, or they may be discomforted by the evident pain. Even if friends respond perfectly, the infertile person may draw back from this source of support. The presence of friends' children may be too painful a reminder. "It became very uncomfortable being around old friends who now had children, hearing talk about kids all the time."[11] Or, realizing that a depressed person is no fun to be with, one may choose not to burden friends with one's gloominess.

Grieving in isolation is disorienting because of the difficulty in measuring the appropriateness of anger and depression. Perspective is lost. The infertile person may fear for his or her sanity. This was or had at one time been a concern among most of those I interviewed.

Accepting Infertility

Yet somehow one survives. And the very fact of having survived creates something positive. One may not be powerful enough to cure infertility, but at least one is tough enough to survive it. This positive turn in self-image is a mark of accepting infertility as a part of the self.

When the infertile person says, "I have put myself through enough pain; if I am infertile, so be it," the person's attention shifts from "Why am I infertile?" to "How am I going to live with being infertile?" This shift is usually a conscious decision. Most infertile persons I talked to remembered the exact moment they shifted direction. Marie was kneeling over the toilet vomiting for the fifth day in a row, a side-effect of an experimental fertility medication, when she decided she had put herself through enough. Jean and Fred were eating dinner quietly when he asked if she would consider adopting. My husband and I decided to quit trying the day after the surgery which completed our medical work-up. Whatever the impetus, at some point each person becomes conscious that a logical stopping place has been reached—that infertility has been established and can be lived with.

The next step in healing comes with the expression, first to oneself and then to others, of feelings about infertility. One may talk to oneself, or write about infertility, or dream about it. Some become able to share with others the anger and pain of infertility. Others are not able, but the distress becomes so evident that a friend insists on knowing what is wrong. Either way, the infertile person talks to someone. The pain and frustrations and shame often pour out; the defenses are gone. This outpouring is cathartic. Feedback that those feelings are not bizarre or unacceptable, that a person is valued notwithstanding infertility, supports the healing process. Acceptance of self, infertility and all, frees up emotional energy that had been invested in protecting one's identity from the insult of infertility. This energy allows better daily functioning and helps to restore a sense of self-worth. The healing process gains momentum, and the depression begins to lighten.

Infertility intrudes less frequently into daily thoughts, confirming the continuing resolution of feelings. When reminders do arise, one copes from the identity of an "infertile person." A twitch in a woman's abdomen is gas, rather than a first sign of pregnancy. Periods start without tears, though still with sadness. One rejoices with a friend who has become pregnant, knowing that she and her husband have been spared the pain.

Because intercourse directly links with procreation, sexual enjoyment is often late to be restored. A year may pass and still thoughts about timing intrude. Two years after my husband and I had halted our medical quest, I surprised myself by desiring sex for the pleasure of it. Years later, during intercourse, thoughts of what might have been still sometimes cloud lovemaking.

Accepting infertility does not mean abandoning all hope. Couples, infertile for years, do occasionally conceive. But such events are rare. Therefore, it is a quiet hope—a bitter-sweet "wouldn't-it-be-nice-if-it-happened-to-me" hope—co-existing with the assumption that a biological child will never happen. Plans and actions are based on that premise. Yet an awareness remains that the experience of pregnancy and the opportunity to pass on the family chin or gift for music was missed.

Implications for Others

The following paragraphs are addressed to the family and friends of a person who is, or possibly is, infertile. You suspect something is wrong. Someone you care about deeply is in pain. You want to help. But when approaching someone who is grieving (and infertile persons are doing exactly that) you "don't know what to say." The following are some dos and don'ts which may aid you in being useful and supportive.

Do start by asking. Start because the infertile person, feeling isolated and ashamed, may hesitate to reach out for help. Part of caring about someone is conquering your own discomfort about possible rebuff and risking an offer of help. Ask, because your assumptions about the situation may be wrong. Perhaps the couple has chosen not to raise children.

If your assumption of an infertility problem is correct, but the person is not ready to talk to you at this time, asking opens the door for the person to come to you later.

Do listen. Listening says, "I care about you. I want to learn about your experience. I am willing to shoulder some of your pain." *Don't offer unsolicited advice,* cheap comfort, reassurances that "it will come out fine in the end," or stories of someone who had it worse. Such comments insult the seriousness of the pain and distance you from the person. Attempts to "make it all better" arise from the listener's own discomfort with the pain of the infertile person. Better the listener should say, "I hurt for you," "It must be rough," or say nothing at all.

Do offer support. Once you have asked and listened, you may want to act. Infertility lowers a person's sense of worth, so comments that show acceptance are supportive. For example, "Now that you explain it, I can understand why you feel that way. I would too." Along with your own comments, a referral to other sources of support may be helpful. Resolve (see p. 39) or a skilled counselor may help an infertile couple. Suggest, but do not push. Meanwhile, don't tear down the person's self-esteem by judging emotions or second-guessing the medical situation. "Maybe you two are trying too hard," or other such advice implies fault. The last thing the infertile person needs is fault-finding.

Do reinforce stressed relationships, for example, between the infertile person and yourself or between the person and the spouse. Say that you are available to listen or help however you can. Drop by, telephone or write—whatever you would normally do to stay in touch. Don't let your friendship deteriorate for lack of contact. (It is easy to do, because the infertile person is not fun to be with while depressed.) To support the person's relationship with spouse, ask how the spouse is faring or comment on how rough it must be on both. Don't ask whose fault it is or encourage the anger the person may be feeling toward the spouse. Remember that both are hurting.

This advice is tough to follow, but do try: *don't be afraid to goof*. Infertile couples I interviewed differentiated between comments that did not come out right, but were said from caring, and those which were thoughtless platitudes. They were grateful for the caring, even if clumsily offered.

3

Choosing
a Physician

Finding the right physician to do the
infertility work-up takes effort. The
first effort is getting started. Having relinquished initial denial
and conceded to the evidence of a fertility problem, one is
ready to consult a doctor. The prospective visit to a doctor
produces mixed feelings. To be infertile is not desired, yet
one wants to have judged the situation correctly. The anxi-
eties, the fear, and the uncertainty which were triggered by
the thought of infertility and have been suffered in the preceding weeks or months are so consuming that it may be a
relief to hear an expert say, "You may have a problem." A
diagnosis of possible infertility is the first step toward obtaining a cure.

But what if the doctor does not confirm an infertility
problem? What if the "diagnosis" is that fears are premature?
The inference of that diagnosis is that the patient has over-
reacted, has succumbed to unwarranted concern—and the
person may feel stupid for it. Perhaps there is a problem,
but if the request for help is premature, if "only time will
tell" (and "time" may be several months to a year, depending
on the doctor), then there is nothing to do but wait until the
doctor, or some doctor, is satisfied that the symptoms of

infertility have been established by the failure to conceive and is ready to begin formal diagnosis. Meanwhile, the fears and tension grow. One worries about infertility and fears that the very act of worrying when it is "premature" is the mark of overconcern bordering on instability. To consult a doctor is to risk having to resurrect the defense of denial which was only just relinquished. Contacting a doctor in spite of this risk requires effort.

Medical Competence

A doctor treating infertile persons needs to be competent in handling both the medical and the emotional components of infertility. By what criteria may a lay person identify a competent doctor? Not all doctors willing to treat infertility problems are medically fit to do so. Several persons I interviewed stressed this point. After a year of diagnostic visits, Bonnie was told by her gynecologist that her cramps and infertility were caused by emotional problems. The doctor suggested that she see a psychiatrist to rid herself of her need to suffer. At the insistence of her mother, this now distraught woman consulted a second gynecologist who, after reviewing Bonnie's medical history, suspected and later surgically confirmed severe endometriosis (a common contributor to infertility often characterized by painful cramping—see Chapter 4). Bonnie's former gynecologist had not kept abreast of recent findings in the field of infertility. He had failed to recognize his limitations or, at least, to explain them to Bonnie. About one third of the infertile couples I talked with had received conflicting diagnoses when they consulted a second physician. Therefore, persons who suspect an infertility problem are advised to choose carefully a physician qualified to treat infertility, and then consider arranging for a second opinion either through that physician or on their own.

Use of the following referral sources may assist in the

search for a fertility specialist. Organizations specializing in infertility problems often provide referrals. For example, Resolve offers a "Directory of Infertility Resources" listing specialists and clinics in the United States. This directory can be obtained by contacting:

Resolve Inc.
P.O. Box 474
Belmont, Massachusetts   02178
(617) 484-2424

The American Fertility Society offers lists of its members by state. Membership indicates that a physician's areas of interest or specialization include infertility. As a member, the physician regularly receives materials describing developments in this rapidly expanding field. A list can be obtained at no cost by writing:

The American Fertility Society
1608 13th Avenue South, Suite 101
Birmingham, Alabama   35256
(205) 933-7222

Local chapters of the American Medical Association will mail or give by telephone the names of two or three area physicians who frequently treat fertility problems.

Local hospitals will often do the same, although most recommend only those doctors who are on their staff.

A family physician is another source of referral. A general practitioner should know of specialists located in the area. A family physician having an interest in fertility problems may begin an infertility work-up, provided that the physician recognizes and can explain his or her abilities and limitations in the area of infertility, is supported through consultation with an infertility specialist, and arranges to refer to that specialist when the need arises.

Other infertile persons form a third source of referral. While societies and colleagues can judge the medical credentials of a specialist, patients are the best source of information about a doctor's compassion, care, ability to explain procedures, and ability to offer support during times of stress. Many infertile couples have had the opportunity to compare doctors while seeking second or more specialized opinions.

Comparison of recommendations from these several sources gives the opportunity to find a competent doctor and the assurance of having chosen as intelligently as possible.

Having chosen a doctor, one may be tempted to assume a passive stance, letting the expert decide the course of diagnosis and treatment. Experts are supposed to know how to determine whatever it is that is wrong (and how to fix that which is amiss). For the patient, understanding the whys and wherefores of infertility testing is a demanding task at a time when the patient has a difficult enough challenge suffering through the testing process and its uncertainties. But even doctors who are well trained and well informed are not always conscientious in their care of patients. If not monitored, some physicians are less careful and thorough. The most blatant story of shoddy medical care I heard came from Marie. She had consulted the fertility specialist at a large metropolitan hospital. The doctor "was too busy to bother with initial physicals and careful histories. Just from looking at me (Marie is boyish in appearance), the doctor was sure that what I needed was this new drug she was researching." Six months and quite a few side-effects later, Marie and her husband consulted a second doctor, who found a likely, though less exotic, explanation for their infertility in the husband's health history.

To aid the reader in monitoring the quality of care being received, Chapter 4 presents a model of an infertility work-up. The model will outline what one might expect during a normal work-up, allaying fears of the unknown; describe various tests, allowing time to formulate questions before arriving at the doctor's office where tension may make thinking difficult; and present for comparison a "standard" infertility work-up, alerting a patient to deviations or omissions in a course of treatment. Not all tests listed are appropriate to every person, as choice of techniques in a given work-up is governed by the results of previous tests and the doctor's observations. Do ask about those tests or results not understood. The doctor's answers provide information concerning the infertility prognosis and also may give an indication of the quality of care being received. Questions alert a conscientious doctor to areas of particular concern to the patient and to aspects of the work-up which require further explanation.

Emotional Competence

A doctor treating infertility should be aware of the emotional as well as the medical aspect of infertility. A doctor's care and competences in dealing with the emotional aspects of patients' experience can help to minimize the stress and emotional scarring suffered by patients. Dr. Sherwin Kaufman highlights physicians' responsibility for their patients' emotional health: "No matter how good the professional qualifications of the specialist consulted, he must above all be sensitive to the special needs of the childless couple. A history of infertility is a history of frustration." [1] Choose the best medical technician available. After the first few visits, decide whether this doctor will offer sufficient emotional support. The following areas of concern may assist in judging a doctor's sensitivity and skill in the emotional area of infertility.

The doctor's first responsibility is to do no harm, either through apathy to the emotional side of infertility, or as a by-product of frustration at the limits of medical science. Doctors who are more interested in the technical challenges of the mechanics of reproduction than in the infertile patient as a person may be insensitive to patients' emotional needs. Other doctors burn out. Constantly exposed to the anxiety and pain of their patients, they protect themselves by developing an emotional callousness and lose their capacity to respond to patients' needs. A doctor's frustration results in damage when, having found no identifiable reason for infertility, the doctor cannot admit the limits of his or her skill or of medical knowledge.

Instead, the doctor may attribute the infertility to the patient's disturbed emotional condition (always the woman's, although men contribute to or are fully responsible medically for half of the cases of infertility). The inability to bear a desperately wanted child, the disruption of frequent, invasive medical tests, and the intrusion of scheduling in sexual relationships combine to produce emotional distress in any infertile woman. A diagnosis that emotional stress is the cause, rather than the result, of infertility can neither be proven nor disproven and so is easily and frequently abused. Experience attests that neither emotional disturbance nor desire to remain childless operates reliably to prevent conception. Unless some specific behavior or biological manifestation of an emotional problem can be identified—as in the case of a woman who had an uncontrollable urge to douche immediately after intercourse—a couple receiving this diagnosis should seek a second opinion.

Thoughtlessness in office hours and arrangements may also result in insult to the vulnerable self-esteem of patients. Gynecologists should provide separate office hours for infertile patients. I found sitting in a waiting room full of pregnant women, all happily reading the *Baby Talk* and *New Mother* magazines available from the magazine rack, excruciating. How desperately I wished to be one of them! My husband was doubly uncomfortable. He was pained at not being a parent-to-be, and he felt awkward being the only male in the waiting room. Doctors who do not keep separate office hours (with alternative reading material) rub salt in open wounds.

The doctor should offer a private space for the man to gather sperm samples. Mike told of being directed by a nurse to the men's washroom—which had no stall doors. Just as he thought he might succeed in producing a sample, another man walked in, gasped, and fled. "I gave up. I told the nurse I'd come back some other time and went home. It took me six months to get up the nerve to return." Offering this man the use of an examining room would have saved him embarrassment and his marriage the stress caused by his refusal for six months to respond to his wife's pleas to continue their infertility work-up.

A doctor's carefulness about details of office arrangements is an indicator of that doctor's general concern about the emotional issues of infertility.

The doctor's second responsibility is to support the patient's emotional health in those areas particularly stressed by infertility. While each person's experience of infertility reflects his or her particular emotional strengths or vulnerabilities, at least four areas of stress are common to all infertile persons. A doctor sensitive to these stress areas can help the patient cope with the emotional experience of infertility.

A person unable to bear a desired baby and disoriented by the chaos of emotions that accompanies medical infertility is a person out of control. The person does not know why infertility is happening, how or whether fertility can be regained, or whether she or he can cope with the accompanying emotions. Being out of control assails one's sense of identity. Sexual identity is challenged by the inability to procreate. Intellectual identity is challenged by the inability to decipher why or how infertility is happening. Identity as an adult is challenged by not knowing how to act sensibly on one's own behalf.

The infertile person may not be able to gain control to alter the infertility, but the person can regain intellectual control by learning the reasons for infertility and rebuild an adult identity by taking an active decision-making role in the treatment of the infertility. The doctor who understands that feeling out of control damages a person's sense of self-worth will support efforts to regain control wherever possible. From the first visit, the patient should be able to find out what tests are used to determine the cause of infertility, what treatments are available for the more common causes, the likelihood of a cure, and at what cost. The expense of monthly office visits for a year or two, laboratory work, and hospital stays can be substantial. Some insurance policies cover some bills. Most doctors are open to patients' requests for a payment plan, because they know it is a financial burden and want patients to be able to complete medical work-ups.

This and all exchanges of information should be two-directional, adult speaking to adult, as contrasted with a one-directional, doctor/authority telling patient what she or he "needs to know." The patient should receive the opportunity and encouragement to solicit information, understand it, and settle doubts. Without such feedback, the doctor may be supplying information which is too sophisticated, too simple, or not pertinent to the patient's concerns. A doctor who spews information at the patient without the benefit of feedback risks patronizing at a time when the patient already feels less than adequate, or leaving unanswered a question at a time when the patient most needs to feel informed. Years after her medical work-up, Sally was haunted by the fear that her doctor had overlooked a pertinent item in her husband's health history. (His former marriage had also been infertile.) Her doctor had never asked if she had questions, and she had been too intimidated to ask.

A sensitive doctor knows it is hard to ask questions of an "expert." A physician may encourage patients in several ways. For example, when asking whether the patient has any questions, he or she should do so in a private room, while everyone is seated and relaxed, thus inviting conversation, rather than during an examination, or while standing with a hand on a doorknob, indicating a desire to leave. (What woman can ask questions comfortably while lying on a gynecologist's table with her feet in stirrups and her knees spread apart!)

A useful first response to any question can be encouragement for having asked, for example, "That's a good question." The response should not be an annoyed or disapproving stare. A doctor should indicate in response to questions that the patient is welcome to ask about anything—even if the question "sounds dumb" or is one which the doctor is unable to answer at the present moment.

One area particularly difficult to discuss for many infertile persons, and more than a few doctors, is sexual habits. This is an important area of information gathering for both infertile persons and doctors. Yet over half of the people I interviewed reported that their doctor asked no questions about their sexual habits beyond whether the woman remained prone after intercourse. Another couple said their doctor spoke with only half his normal volume when asking questions concerning sex, "like a kid whispering about something dirty." My physician often asked rhetorical questions, for example, "You did have intercourse twice last week, didn't you?" I was hesitant to disagree with him when we had done something different than what he described with his "questions." Such behavior stands in stark contrast to a second doctor I consulted. He joked comfortably about his own embarrassment at having to ask such personal questions. (He said he practiced asking his wife until he could do so without blushing.) Then he proceeded to ask questions in a matter-of-fact way.

If a doctor asks no questions about sexual activity during the initial physical, an integral part of an infertility history has been omitted. Ask about this omission.

While it is the doctor's responsibility to encourage questions, both verbally and nonverbally, it is the patient's responsibility to ask. Asking questions may be difficult. One fears distracting the doctor from the all-important task of achieving pregnancy, or provoking the doctor into confirming the hidden worry that emotional problems are interfering with conception. One may fear discovering the doctor's limitations in ability to cure infertility.

Ask anyway. If the doctor does not welcome questions, it is better to discover this immediately and consider selecting another physician who does. It is easier to change doctors before having invested a lot of time, trust, and money in the first physician's care. The exchange of information is a process in which both doctor and patient should be involved. A sensitive doctor appreciates the patient's need to know and will take care to explain without resorting to medical jargon or rushing the patient.

The next step toward gaining control of the situation is to participate in the decision-making process concerning the course of diagnosis and treatment. Informed patient participation is sensible because, as the work-up proceeds, more decisions become discretionary.

Some doctors encourage patients to assume a passive stance and to leave decisions to the doctor's discretion. "Who's the doctor here anyway?" chided Mark's physician. Another said, "Don't worry your pretty little head about it. I'll do the worrying for both of us. You just follow the directions and relax."

Interactions with such a doctor can be seductive. The doctor sounds confident and in control of the problem for which the patient feels so out of control. But as months pass and no pregnancy occurs, the patient begins to feel deceived or betrayed. Now distrustful, the patient may try to ask questions or give feedback. But such doctors rarely are able or willing to listen. Having had trust betrayed by the doctor's mishandling of the emotional aspect of infertility, the patient often begins wondering whether the doctor has misrepresented medical skills also. The doctor may be offended by the affront to expertise which the patient's now hostile questions represent. The patient becomes more and more suspicious of the doctor's motives and abilities. Neither clearly expresses these feelings to the other. The patient may break off treatment abruptly. Marie and Al stopped treatment, suddenly, after two years of monthly visits and unquestioning obedience to the doctor's instructions. "We had absorbed enough pain and spent enough time and money getting nowhere." Their doctor's response was, "Well, some people want children and some don't." The anger of undiscussed feelings shows on both sides of this exchange.

A doctor should involve patients in decision making by

offering information, soliciting questions, and explaining options. The patient should respond by asking questions, considering the options presented, and informing the doctor of choices or preferences. Participating in decision making may be difficult and painful. Often no "right answer" exists. Instead, one must measure the risks, discomfort, and cost of proceeding with particular testing or treatment against the need to know the cause of one's infertility or to try all possible avenues, however remote, to achieve pregnancy. Infertility work is elective. Each person should proceed at the pace and to the extent that meets individual needs.

A doctor can be particularly helpful to the patient in identifying the point at which she or he is ready to accept infertility as a probable permanent condition, end medical pursuit, and begin considering alternatives. The comfort and confidence of a good patient/physician relationship is illustrated by Lea's comment: "I asked our doctor to tell us when we have completed a reasonable medical course. I know she will; she has always been straightforward with us." If a doctor does not encourage active patient involvement in the decision-making process, the patient can insist, change doctors, or suffer the frustration.

A person in the process of adjusting to infertility progresses through predictable emotional stages. A doctor treating infertility should be cognizant of these stages. The doctor should monitor the patient's progress by asking about and observing emotions. The doctor can anticipate expressions of pain and anger. Time spent compassionately listening may be more valuable to the patient than any advice or treatment the doctor can offer. The patient comes for medical help, but the patient is dealing with emotional trauma as well. There may be no one other than the doctor to whom the patient is willing to express these concerns and feelings. Every doctor should have a box of tissue on the office desk for patients to wipe the tears of frustration provoked by yet another intrusive, inconclusive medical test. A doctor bolsters the patient's sense of self-worth by being willing to sit with the person through such painful moments.

A doctor should accept expressions of physical pain, also. Some tests hurt. I cringed as the doctor inflated my blocked tubes, and at one point had to ask him to stop so I could cope with the pain. Afterwards he said, "That wasn't so bad now, was it?" How could I say, "Yes, it was!" He had already made light of my pain. I felt like a crybaby. If he had said, "Sorry that had to hurt," I could have told him it was excruciating, which it was, and still felt like I had some human dignity. A doctor confirms a patient's beleaguered sense of worth by being willing to tolerate and acknowledge expressions of physical pain. The patient builds no personal hostility at the doctor for inflicting that pain, because the doctor has made his or her concern clear.

Along with monitoring emotional progress and accepting expressions of emotions, the doctor should educate the patient about the emotional stages of infertility. While the doctor may know from experience that infertile patients suffer anger and depression, the patient may not realize that these emotions are expected and normal. Many couples I interviewed would have been spared much anguish if their physicians had taken a few minutes to explain that these powerful emotions are a normal, even necessary, component of infertility.

Most doctors have neither the skill nor the time to support or educate patients in depth concerning the stages of infertility. Doctors should, therefore, offer referral sources for further help, to be used at the patient's discretion. To provide such referrals may require that the doctor actively seek out or help to create such sources. Large fertility centers can provide in-house counseling services.[2] A doctor in private practice or at a smaller center might check with local mental-health or family-counseling centers. Resolve provides literature for doctors' offices explaining their services. Every doctor can maintain a small lending library for laypersons on the medical and emotional aspect of infertility. (See bibliography for suggestions.)

If a doctor fails to ask about emotional well-being or to refer to sources of emotional support, the patient should ask about this omission. If the doctor does not educate patients about the emotional aspect of infertility, then the patient can educate the doctor or go elsewhere.

An infertile person is half of a couple under siege. Presumably both spouses want a child (if not, a referral for counseling is appropriate). Both are childless, regardless of which is found to be medically infertile. Both individuals are frustrated by their inability to have that desired child.

Not only are two individuals assaulted by infertility, but so is their relationship. A person depleted by the anguish of infertility has less energy to give to relationships with others. The stress of wondering who is at fault results in a mixture of guilt ("I've deprived my spouse of children") and anger ("It must be my spouse's fault"). Regulated and timed sex takes the romance out of "lovemaking," further stressing the relationship. If for either spouse a major purpose of marriage was to have children, then infertility may challenge the foundation of the marriage.

A doctor should view the infertile patient not only as an individual, but also as half of a couple. The wife is usually the initiator of the search for medical help, but the doctor should request that the husband be present from the first visit. Including both spouses at the initiation of the medical investigation affirms that both are involved in and suffering from the condition of infertility, regardless of which spouse may eventually be found medically infertile. This procedure is also medically sound (see Chapter 4).

A doctor should continue to confer with both spouses frequently during the investigation, even if one is clearly responsible medically for the infertility. Only then can the doctor offer both spouses ongoing medical information, rudimentary emotional support, and referral (as a couple) for further supportive counseling. Bonnie's doctor was able to do very helpful basic counseling because he had continued to observe both spouses together throughout their work-up, although the medical problem was Bonnie's alone. "The doctor talked with me and my husband separately one month and together the next. He urged us to stop trying to blame each other and face this together. He probably saved our marriage. I know he saved my sanity."

The infertile couple should insist that a doctor treat them as a single unit as well as two individuals. Decisions regarding the course of investigation and treatment should ordinarily be the decisions of the couple, not only of the individual who is medically "culpable."

Hope for a cure is probably the most complex emotion with which both patient and physician must contend. Each treatment brings hope and each period disappointment. The patient rides an emotional roller coaster. The doctor's most casual comment may exert a powerful influence on the patient's outlook because the patient is unsure how much hope is realistic.

A doctor who never mentions hope fails to recognize the patient's need for the sustaining power of realistic hope. Over half of those who seek medical help do achieve pregnancy. Hope is the counterweight to the fear and depression felt toward the equally realistic possibility that the infertile person may never give birth to a child.

A doctor who is excessively hopeful mocks the patient's recognition of this second reality and is usually a doctor who has difficulty facing the limitations of medicine in curing infertility. The doctor denies to the patient and to her or himself that the infertility may be insoluble. Terry said, "The first time the doctor said, 'This really looks good,' my spirits soared. I thought, *Finally, I'm going to get pregnant.* A month later when he said, 'This time things really look good,' I believed him again. But the third month I heard, 'This looks really hopeful,' I was skeptical. And by the fourth month it sounded hollow." Such a doctor loses credibility.

Seek a doctor who seems to offer hope realistically. If one can trust a doctor's words concerning the likelihood of achieving a pregnancy, then when the doctor suggests proceeding with medical testing or treatment, the patient is sustained by the doctor's hope for success. And when the doctor suggests that everything medically reasonable has been done, the patient knows that the time has come to consider alternatives to a biological child, or to consult a different physician.

A doctor may or may not be able to alter medical infertility, but he or she will always influence the person's emotional experience during the months of medical diagnosis and treatment. Seek a competent medical technician who has sufficient sensitivity to emotional issues to give support. If the first physician consulted proves not to be adequate in both areas, consider choosing another. The search may be frustrating, but when I asked those I interviewed what they would do differently, 75 percent answered that they would have taken the time and put forth the effort to find a more medically and emotionally competent doctor. Added Sandi, "Tell people that it is a lot easier to change doctors after the first few visits than ten months later. We changed later and had to repeat many tests we had just suffered through a few months earlier. But it was worth it. Our current physician found several medical problems his predecessor missed, and he is so much easier to talk to."

4

A Model
of a Medical
Work-Up

A medical work-up begins with a phone call, usually by the woman to a gynecologist who specializes in infertility. The woman is asked the general nature of the problem and an appointment time is set. Some physicians mail the couple a questionnaire to be completed before the first office visit. This allows the couple to review their medical history at home with records available and without the anxiety of being in a doctor's office. Do not be surprised if a specialist has a long waiting list for new patients.

The First Visit

At the first visit the doctor will ask each spouse about general health history, history of sexual development (for example, the onset of menstruation or the occurrence of postpubescent mumps in the man), and current sexual functioning (including characteristics of the woman's menses and frequency of intercourse). The doctor will examine both individuals physically, including a pelvic exam for the woman and a genital exam for the man. (Some gynecologists refer the man to a urologist for this examination and for evaluation of general health and fertility.) Individual exams offer a chance for either spouse to mention, in privacy, aspects of medical or sexual history which might be embarrassing to discuss in the presence of the other. Blood may be drawn for testing. If the woman has not had German measles (rubella), the doctor may inoculate to eliminate the risk to a fetus.

During this visit, the doctor will explain the Basal Temperature Graph, a technique used to establish the woman's pattern of ovulation. The woman takes her temperature each morning before getting out of bed and records the results. The graph's utility is based on the fact that estrogen is the predominant hormone during the first half of a menstrual cycle, while progesterone becomes the dominant hormone as soon as the woman ovulates. Progesterone causes an increase in body temperature. Therefore a "spike," a sudden increase of .5° to 1°, indicates ovulation. Dips in the graph, unless followed by this rise, are insignificant. A graph which shows no definite rise is inconclusive. The woman may not be ovulating or, if she is, her temperature is not following her hormones. Further testing will be necessary.

The man will probably be asked for a sperm sample after an abstinence of two days. (Abstaining longer than two days will not increase potency; abstaining for several weeks or longer may slightly decrease potency.) He masturbates and collects the sample in an examining room, using a container provided by the doctor. Doctors who do not have facilities available to test sperm samples may send the man directly to a lab to collect the sample there and have it processed. Double-check appointment time and procedures with the lab before going. If a man has religious convictions which prohibit masturbation, he should discuss this with the doctor. Some allow the collection of a sperm sample at home using a dry condom designed for sperm collection during intercourse. (The sperm count will not be accurate if a condom with a lubricant is used or if the sample is collected after withdrawal [coitus interruptus]. The lubricants on condoms kill sperm. Before withdrawal, some fluid leaks out and this first fluid contains a significant number of sperm.) Doctors disagree whether the dry condom method yields an accurate, uncontaminated sample, and some laboratories will not accept such a sample. There is also a procedure by which a urologist can draw a sperm sample without ejaculation. Sperm samples should be tested within an hour, so sperm collected at home must be rushed to the doctor's office or laboratory. Sperm tests often must be repeated because the laboratory work involved is delicate, open to about a twenty percent error rate with a good technician, and because a single abnormal result may be caused by a variety of temporary factors, such as a recent bout with the flu.[1]

The doctor will suggest that the couple have intercourse every other or every third day for the ten days centered around the time that the woman's temperature should spike, assuming that it has spiked in previous months. No hot baths for the man, because the heat can harm sperm. Boxer rather than jockey shorts may be suggested because the latter prevent the testicles from descending away from excessive body heat. Also, no pot smoking, because smoking marijuana may reduce both sperm count and sperm motility.

The Woman's Work-Up

Assuming the man's sperm count is normal, subsequent testing for the woman may include the following:

1. A vaginal examination on the tenth, fourteenth, and eighteenth day of her cycle, assuming a 28-day cycle, to check the quantity and quality of the mucus. The high estrogen content of the mucus before ovulation gives it different characteristics than after ovulation. Immediately preceding ovulation the mucus is elastic and can be stretched, like hot pizza cheese. (This elasticity is called spinnbarkeit.) Also, before ovulation the mucus should form a fern-like pattern when pressed between two glass slides. The doctor may juxtapose these results with the Basal Temperature Chart to further

check ovulation patterns. Some problems in hormone balance may be corrected with medication. If there is an unusually large quantity of mucus or any indication of infection, the doctor may check for the acidity/alkalinity balance of the mucus. The procedure is similar to a pap smear. If the doctor takes a sample of mucus from the mouth (os) of the cervix, the woman may feel a slightly different sensation, like a slight pinch or poke; it is not painful.

2. An endometrium biopsy tells the doctor whether ovulation has or has not occurred. It also alerts the doctor to a probable luteal phase defect, a slight progesterone imbalance which occurs in three to five percent of infertile women. (Endometrium tissue lines the inside of the uterus; part of this tissue is shed during menstruation.) This test may be part of the eighteenth-day vaginal exam, although many doctors prefer to be closer to day 25 of a 28-day cycle. The doctor may dilate the cervix slightly by inserting thin tubes, starting at the width of a pencil lead and progressing to about a half inch in diameter, or the doctor may be able to use a speculum alone. (The speculum is the instrument used during a pap smear to open up the vagina and allow the doctor to look at the cervix.) Through the cervix the doctor inserts a thin rod with a tiny flat loop at the end, and scrapes a few cells off the uterine lining. No anesthetic is necessary. The process may take from a few minutes to a half hour and may cause negligible to severe temporary cramping, depending on the tenseness of the cervix and the skill of the doctor. If a luteal phase defect is indicated by the results of the first biopsy, a second is necessary to confirm this diagnosis. The progesterone imbalance can be corrected with medication. (An endometrium biopsy has nothing to do with the diagnosing of endometriosis.)

3. A post-coital examination (Sim-Huhner test) checks the survival rate and motility of sperm in the cervical mucus. The woman is seen in mid-cycle (ovulation time), two to four hours after intercourse. This procedure is similar to a pap smear. If the doctor does not find a normal number of live,

moving sperm in the cervical mucus, the test is repeated, because a single negative result is not conclusive. If a low sperm count or low activity level is found again, the doctor may prescribe medication to alter the cervical mucus. A few women may produce antibodies which kill the sperm. Research on this possibility is just beginning. If the doctor suspects this, he or she may recommend "condom therapy." (The man wears a condom during sexual intercourse for about six months to let the woman's vagina desensitize to sperm. Then the couple tries to conceive.) If this fails, the woman may be artificially inseminated with her husband's sperm in order to bypass the vaginal and cervical mucus. The sperm is injected into the uterus, using a syringe with a thin tube rather than a needle. The procedure is not uncomfortable. The doctor will probably ask that the woman remain prone for 20 minutes, so the sperm do not drain out of the uterus. Insemination may be repeated two or three times around each ovulation, for up to six ovulatory cycles, because fertile couples frequently require up to six months to conceive.

4. Utero-tubal insufflation (Rubin test) or "having one's tubes blown" indicates whether the Fallopian tubes are obstructed. The doctor pumps carbon dioxide into the uterus through a thin tube inserted vaginally. The woman then sits up. If gas escapes through the tubes and into the abdominal cavity, the woman's shoulders will begin to ache. That escape of gas indicates that at least one tube is open. The gauge on the carbon dioxide pump tells the doctor how much pressure was required, further indicating the likelihood of partial or complete blockage of the tubes. If the woman's tubes are not open normally, the pressure of the gas in the uterus may cause painful, though temporary cramping. The ache of the shoulders may also be quite uncomfortable for the next half hour, until the gas is absorbed into the blood stream and passed out through the lungs. This procedure is sometimes repeated in women with partially blocked tubes in an effort to force the Fallopian tubes to remain open.

A hysterosalpingogram is an alternative procedure for ascertaining whether the Fallopian tubes are open. Radiopaque dye is injected vaginally through a thin tube into the uterus and an X-ray is taken, to learn if the dye is flowing out from the uterus through one or both tubes. The dye is water-soluble and is eventually absorbed by the body and passed in the urine. This procedure may also be used therapeutically in an attempt to keep the tubes open. The pressure of the dye in the uterus may cause temporary cramping, especially in women whose tubes are partially or wholly blocked. This procedure is preferred by many physicians because they can actually see the tubes "fill and spill" and can distinguish whether one or both tubes are open. Also, many physicians report that a hysterosalpingogram is less uncomfortable for most women than a utero-tubal insufflation.

If a woman's tubes are irreparably blocked or damaged, but ovulation, womb and husband's sperm are normal, in vitro fertilization may be possible. A ripe egg is surgically removed from an ovary, united with sperm in the laboratory, and then implanted in the womb ("test tube baby"). This technique is expensive and available at only a few infertility centers; a couple pursuing this option may have to wait several years if accepted. Locations of infertility centers performing this procedure may be obtained by writing Resolve or the American Fertility Society (see p. 39).

5. A laparoscopy allows a doctor to look directly at the Fallopian tubes and the ovaries. The woman is given a general anesthetic. The doctor makes a small incision at the navel and inserts a laparoscope—a thin tube lined with reflecting filaments. The Fallopian tubes and ovaries are examined for congenital deformity or damage from disease. A biopsy of an ovary may be done. If the doctor thinks a biopsy is indicated, he or she will explain this to the patient ahead of time and ask the patient to sign the required consent forms. Minor repair surgery such as the removal of a benign cyst from a tube is also possible.

The doctor may make a second tiny incision at about the

pubic hairline to do a biopsy for endometriosis, a condition in which endometrian tissue has grown outside the interior of the uterus, in the pelvic cavity. Endometriosis may cause severe cramping, extra bleeding during periods (because the endometrian tissue bleeds during periods regardless of where it is located) and pain during intercourse for some women. For other women, there will be no symptoms. Sometimes a doctor suspects endometriosis because of the woman's symptoms, and the laparoscopy often provides confirmation; endometriosis is a common contributor to infertility. In the 20 percent of women for whom no cause of infertility has been identified prior to this point and who exhibit no symptoms, the laparoscopy will reveal endometriosis in 16 to 38 percent.[2] The initial treatment for this condition is Danozol (or Danacrine), a synthetic male hormone given in pill form which atrophies the tissue. If medication does not correct the condition within six months, surgery may be necessary to remove the abnormal tissue. Laser surgery techniques have proven effective in some cases.

Since the cervix must be dilated to allow the doctor to move the uterus and look underneath with the laparoscope for endometriosis, most doctors do a D&C (dilate and curettage) at the same time. Cells from the tissue can then be examined in the laboratory for abnormality.

If the woman's insurance covers such a hospital stay, the doctor may do expensive lab work at this point, such as certain hormonal studies, if such are indicated by the woman's history or other test results. The woman goes home later that day or the next day with a small bandage or two on her tummy and grogginess due to the anesthetic.

A culdoscopy is an alternative means for the doctor to look at the condition of the tubes and ovaries. The woman is awake although usually sedated. She assumes a knees-to-chest position, bottom in the air. Local anesthetic numbs the pelvic area and a culdoscope (the forerunner of the laparoscope in the United States) is inserted through a small incision made in the vaginal wall, into the pelvic cavity. A culdoscope does not allow the physician as wide a visual field and requires more skill to use properly than a laparoscope.

The Man's Work-Up

If a man's sperm count is not normal, he will be tested further. The semen sample may be abnormal in that the volume of fluid is low, the sperm are less active than normal (poor motility), the live sperm count is low (oligospermia), or there may be no live sperm (azoospermia). If the fertility specialist is a gynecologist, the man will be referred to a urologist. The urologist initially reviews the man's health history and does a physical. Part of the physical will include:

1. An examination for varicocele, which is a varicosity of the vein in the spermatic cord. The incidence is 15 percent in the general population; 40 percent among infertile males.[3] Surgery to tie off and remove the vein often significantly increases sperm count and sperm motility. The procedure requires a one-day hospital stay because a general anesthetic is used.

Further testing may include the following:

2. An endocrine or hormone analysis, checking for imbalances which occur in ten percent of males with infertility problems.[4] Testing requires a blood sample.

3. A vasogram, a test which tells the doctor whether the vas deferens is open. The vas deferens is the Y-shaped tube that conveys sperm from the testicles to the tip of the penis. This test is indicated if the doctor suspects a blockage. A small incision is made in the scrotum and radiopaque dye is injected with a syringe into the vas deferens. An X-ray shows whether the dye is passing through the tubing. The procedure is the male equivalent to the hysterosalpingogram. A local anesthetic is used, and the vasogram performed on an outpatient basis, unless the patient requests a general anesthetic. Blockage of the vas deferens may be surgically corrected or bypassed.

4. A testicular biopsy, a means of learning whether testicles are producing sperm. This test is indicated if the doctor suspects failure of the testicles to function. The doctor makes a small incision in the scrotum and shaves off a very thin slice from a testicle (enough for a microscopic slide). The biopsy procedure may be done in the doctor's office, using a local anesthetic, or in a hospital using a general anesthetic if the man so requests. If the biopsy indicates that the testicles are not producing sperm, little can be done to correct the problem.

In about five percent of males, no cause for infertility can be diagnosed.[5]

Reasonable Expectations

A patient should understand the reason for and the logistics of any procedure before undergoing it. Often seeing the instruments involved is helpful. If equipment is not routinely presented and explained beforehand, ask the doctor or nurse to do so.

The total medical work-up and treatment may take anywhere from several months to several years. Assuming no cause is yet found, a woman should undergo the hysterosalpingogram (or utero-tubal insufflation) by about the third month of investigation. The doctor may then halt visits for three to six months because of the high incidence of pregnancy after these procedures. Assuming no success, the doctor does a laparoscopy (or culdoscopy). For 85-90% of couples, one or more causes are diagnosed. For the other 10-15%, no adequate explanation is found. Within a year of starting their medical work-up the couple should have some diagnosis, or the information that none can be found by the doctor.

Fertility diagnosis and treatment is a developing area of science. For about 60% of couples, a physician is able to help. Thirty years ago the success rate was only 20%.[6] For those interested in keeping abreast of developments, Resolve (see p. 39) sends its members a semimonthly newsletter. The

American Fertility Society (see p. 39) makes available pamphlets on a variety of subjects related to human reproduction and medical advancements in this area, and also publishes a journal for physicians, *Fertility and Sterility*, which is available from some public libraries.

The bibliography lists books containing more detailed information for the layperson on the history and various components of an infertility work-up.

5

Options:
Acting on the
New Assumption

At the point when one stops asking,
"Why am I infertile?" and starts ask-
ing "How am I going to live with it?" what are the options?

Childlessness

One option is to remain childless. For some people having
children by adoption is not acceptable. Robin said, "I didn't
want to raise someone else's child." For Robin, an adopted
child would always have been a second-best substitute. If passing on family characteristics or experiencing pregnancy is para-
mount, then remaining childless may be preferable to any
other alternative.

Others are tired. Having invested several years, a lot of
emotional energy, and a great deal of money into unsuccessful
infertility testing and treatment, a couple may not be willing
to risk more time, emotional energy, and money into trying—
perhaps unsuccessfully—to adopt.

Having chosen this option, both spouses need to have satisfactory role alternatives to parenting. Often the husband
already has a career, but the wife holds a less challenging job

at which she had planned to work until the children came. I talked to three couples who had chosen this option. In each, the wife had returned to school for career-oriented training to develop the skills necessary to enter a more challenging profession.

Other couples choose to remain childless because childlessness is acceptable to them. Mary said, "I did not feel strongly that bearing a child was a requirement for my happiness." Or as another couple told me, "We aren't using birth control (and have not been for three years). If we get pregnant, that would be great. But if we don't that's okay too. We have a good life together. We don't want kids badly enough to put ourselves through infertility testing or the application process for adoption."

Couples who choose to remain childless should prepare themselves for comments such as "When are you two going to have kids?" Lea told people, "We are trying, and seeing a specialist." It was important to her that friends knew she wanted children. Others, feeling less need to explain, develop more abrupt replies.

Adoption

To adopt a baby is a second option. One may not experience pregnancy or pass on genes, but at least one has a baby to cuddle and love. As Ellen said, "Pregnancy lasts nine months, but parenting lasts a lifetime. The baby may not have the family features, but she will have the family values and manners."

Adopting an infant requires perseverance and luck. Since the late 1960s, with the growing acceptability of single women keeping their babies and the increasing incidence of abortion, fewer and fewer healthy infants, especially white infants, are available for adoption.

A child may be adopted privately or through an adoption agency. Private adoptions, unless between relatives, often occur through a physician. Some doctors feel that helping couples adopt is part of their responsibility as infertility specialists. When medical diagnosis and treatment are exhausted, "it is the physician's duty," says Dr. Kaufman, "to help the couple make an emotional adjustment. Advice and help in adopting a child has been the best therapy for many such couples." [1] If one is fortunate enough to have such a doctor, who is trustworthy and who happens to have access to a baby at that moment, adoption through a doctor is possible.

Bonnie suffered endometriosis for years. She had undergone several surgical procedures in her attempt to get pregnant. She had succeeded once, only to miscarry. Finally, she required a hysterectomy. For this woman who loved children, the miscarriage had forced an adjustment to the likelihood of infertility; the subsequent hysterectomy settled the matter. The day after the hysterectomy, her doctor walked in to her hospital room to announce that a newborn was available. Later the doctor said, "You never saw anyone recover from surgery so fast in your life. Of course her husband helped a lot those first few months."

A doctor arranging adoptions has total discretionary power over which child is offered to which couple. A couple considering adopting through a doctor should ask by what criteria the doctor matches babies to potential parents, and then consider whether these criteria meet their needs. If the doctor concentrates on close ethnic matches, but the couple is concerned about the intelligence of the biological parents, then the couple may need to go elsewhere.

A doctor arranging adoptions is operating outside of his or her field of expertise. The advice a doctor gives an adopting couple may or may not be sound, in terms of their psychological adjustment or the baby's future emotional growth. One doctor I know of advised strongly against telling the child of the adoption or even mentioning the word "adopt" unless the child specifically asked. This was the advice of some mental-health experts 50 years ago, but no longer. Such secretiveness has been shown to do children emotional harm.

A couple adopting privately needs to educate themselves to the special emotional needs of adopted children and of adopting parents (see pp. 108-110 for suggestions).

A few doctors arranging adoptions are unethical. Some are careless, like the doctor who accidentally mentioned the biological mother's name while describing a baby to an infertile couple. One wonders if he might not make a similar slip while reassuring the biological mother that her baby would be well cared for. Others are dishonest. The couple should discuss fees with a doctor before signing anything. Potential parents often pay the biological mother's medical expenses and doctor's fees. A disreputable doctor may charge a "finder's fee" under the guise of exorbitant doctor's fees for the birthmother's care.

A couple should get a lawyer before signing or paying for anything. The doctor's first responsibility is to the baby, then to the biological mother if she is under the doctor's care, and then to adopting parents. The couple should have an advocate of their own who knows the mechanics and requirements of adoption proceedings. A lawyer is needed eventually anyway to do the court work involved in adopting. Discuss fees and services ahead of time with the lawyer too. Many lawyers who handle adoptions frequently have a set fee for this service.

Finally, a doctor arranging an adoption chooses which information to give adopting parents concerning the baby and what, if any, to keep in a sealed file. Adopting parents should ask for any details which the doctor can give without actually revealing the biological parents' identity. Health histories alert parents to possible medical problems. Personal and family information will allow parents to better answer their adopted child's eventual questions. Adopting parents might request that the doctor create a sealed file regarding the child, containing names, medical histories, and all other information known to the doctor relating to the biological parents which is too specific to give to the adopting parents. Such a file can be held by the doctor or the lawyer handling the adoption, to be available to the child's pediatrician should medical problems or some other need for history arise, after the physician arranging the adoption has forgotten details or is no longer available.

Private adoptions account for half of the children adopted outside of their extended family in the United States. (Seventy-five percent of independent adoptions are by blood relatives or stepparents.) Agency adoptions account for the other 50%.[2] The first step toward an agency adoption is to compile a comprehensive list of the adoption agencies in the area. Gynecologists, hospital social workers, and maternity homes often have such lists. Check the Yellow Pages. National organizations that refer would-be parents to adoption sources include the following:

North American Center for Adoption
(Division of the Child Welfare League)
67 Irving Place
New York, New York   10003
(212) 254-7410

National Committee for Adoption
1346 Connecticut Avenue N.W., Suite 326
Washington, D.C.   20036
National Adoption Hotline: (202) 463-7563

If adopting a foreign-born child is acceptable, sources for referral include:

The National Committee for Adoption Hotline
(see above)

International Social Services
291 Broadway
New York, New York   10007
(212) 964-7550

OURS
3307 Highway 100 North, Suite 203
Minneapolis, Minnesota   55422
(612) 535-4829

Los Ninos International
1106 Random Circle
Austin, Texas   78745
(512) 443-2833

Call every agency and ask whether they are currently accepting applications. Agencies overwhelmed by applicants often close their doors to prospective parents for several months at a time. The first seven that I telephoned were "closed." Assuming one has the option to choose between several "open," or soon to "open" agencies, the following are criteria to consider:

1. Can we meet the agency's initial requirements? Typical requirements might include that both spouses be between the ages of 21 and 37, have been married to each other for three years, be financially self-supporting, and have a letter from a doctor stating that the couple has completed a full infertility work-up. This last requirement is based on the policy judgment of most agencies that, at a time when the number of children available for adoption is far exceeded by the number of prospective adoptive parents, infertile couples should take priority over those couples who could bear children.

2. How long are the waits? How long is the waiting list to begin applying for an adoption? Agencies that do not close their intake periodically may have a wait of a year before they begin considering a couple's application. How long is the process of application? Agencies that have a detailed application process may take six months or longer to decide whether to accept an applicant. How long is the average wait between being accepted and receiving a child? Some agencies routinely place within a year; these are agencies that limit the number of applicants they will consider according to the number of

babies available for placement. Other agencies, which keep applications open and accept all qualified couples, may have waiting lists of three or even five years. At the few agencies which use the lottery system a couple may wait a month or forever.

3. How much does the agency charge for an adoption? Fees range from no charge (such agencies live on an endowment and donations) to an agency which requires a "donation" of $10,000. Many agencies charge the couple the average cost to the agency of placing a child. Their costs often include the birth mother's medical expenses and counseling costs, the cost of social workers who screen applicants, and the cost of caring for the child from birth to placement. Their fees are usually several thousand dollars. The couple applying to agencies must consider their budget and whether they think a particular fee to be excessive even if they can afford it.

4. Which agencies should be considered? The couple should request and complete initial application forms for any and all agencies they might consider using. This extra investment of time and effort keeps options open.

5. Make initial visits to as many agencies as possible. During the first interview, ask about agency procedures. Understanding what to anticipate during the application process helps avoid unpleasant surprises later. Inquire also about the agency criteria for matching babies and prospective parents. Some agencies solicit the couple's concerns and desires about a baby and try to match the baby to the wants and needs of that couple. Other agencies have relatively inflexible matching criteria—for example, ethnic similarity of child to applicant —which the agency will apply even though the couple would prefer the matching be done on some other basis—for example, quality of prenatal care. If the criteria of the agency do not meet the desires of the couple, the couple should consider other agencies, if possible. Try to meet the social worker who will be processing the application. Good rapport with the social worker will lessen the stress of the adoption process; there will be many hours of interviews, conversation and

questions. If the couple is comfortable with the social worker, the worker is more likely to feel comfortable with the couple, thereby increasing the probability of acceptance by the agency.

After the initial interview (s), most agencies will ask a couple if they wish to pursue the adoption process at that agency. Agencies usually insist that the couple work through only one agency at a time, so that an agency does not invest time and expense in a couple who quite possibly will receive a child through another agency.

With all the interviews and the forms and questions that follow, most agencies are making logical inquiries which require an extended period of observation and discussion. Agencies seek couples who have finished grieving for their lost fertility and for their "assumption child." An adult who does not accept him or herself totally, including the infertile part, will not be able to accept totally a child whose very presence reminds the adult of that infertility. An adopted child will ultimately have to resolve the insult of rejection by the biological parents. (Having been surrendered for adoption by one's birth-mother feels like rejection to a child, regardless of the birth-mother's motives.) It would be unfair to the child to compound that rejection by placement with adoptive parents who consider him or her a "second-best" substitute for a birthed child.

Agencies look for a healthy working marriage in which partners talk to each other, respect each other's needs, and share each other's hopes—a marriage which has enough extra emotional strength to absorb, withstand, and enjoy a new baby, and to accept whatever additional pressures and impositions family or community may generate because the adopted child is "different" from a biological child.

Agencies consider a couple's support system. Does the couple have family and friends who know of the infertility and plans for adoption and find this acceptable? Will these friends be available to help the couple struggle through the rigors and adjustments of caring for a new baby? Raising a child is demanding and cannot be done in isolation. But, as previously mentioned, infertile couples often have isolated themselves. Reestablishing support systems means going to family and friends, who do not already know, and explaining plans to adopt. Such explanations engender questions about why the couple is adopting, so the infertility must also be explained. As others learn of the pain which the couple has suffered, they can better appreciate and share the couple's joy if a new baby arrives. Having reestablished contact and trust, the couple can call on friends to help with the trials of parenting. The agency we used encouraged our sharing by requiring of us recommendations from our parents and several friends. This forced us to explain our situation—something which at the time I still found difficult to discuss. These explanations not only helped us marshal our support systems, but also helped me accept more completely our infertility.

Those agencies which have not set matching guidelines to be applied in all cases explore with the couple the characteristics the couple hopes for in a child. Is the couple more concerned that the child should look like she or he could be their biological child, or that the child had good prenatal care, or intelligent parents, or some other aspect? Would the couple consider a physically or mentally handicapped child, or a child who is "legal risk"? (Legal risk means that one, or both, biological parents have failed to sign release forms consenting to the child's adoption.) With few normal, healthy infants available, a couple needs to weigh the importance of their criteria against the length of time they may have to wait for a child who satisfies those criteria.

Some agencies offer counseling at this point, sharing with the couple the experiences of others who have adopted a child of a different race or with a handicap. If a couple adopts a child who does not look like a biological child, the couple needs to be completely comfortable with having adopted, because everyone from family to strangers will notice and many will feel free to comment. Strangers will ask questions like, "Is she yours?" "Is your husband black [or Mexican or whatever]?" "What a wonderful thing you've done!"

(Implication: to take a substandard child) or "Did you know that child is Oriental?" (asked of Julia by a total stranger in front of their six-year-old adopted Korean daughter). These parents must deal frequently with the child's concern about being so different that strangers stare or make comment, and do so with such total acceptance of the child that the child may accept him or herself. Biracial children are not accepted in some neighborhoods; adopting a biracial child may restrict the parents' choice of residence. Some agencies offer groups for parents and children, or just for older children, providing an opportunity for discussion about adopting or being adopted with others who share this identity.

The process of applying for adoption can be discouraging, annoying, and unsettling. Discouraging, because of the knowledge that the agency has too many applicants for too few babies, so some applicants must be rejected. Annoying, because the process is dictated by the agency and must be submitted to. Unsettling, because a decision of great importance rests in the hands of a stranger, and because the "wrong" answer may—one fears—make the difference between a baby and no baby. Those feelings of being out of control which marked the beginning stages of infertility may arise again because new anger often causes old, unresolved anger to resurface. I remember ranting around the house one evening, having just spent several hours getting fingerprinted to meet a state requirement of confirmation that I was not a convicted child abuser. Intellectually, I understood; emotionally, I was furious. "Why me! Why do I have to go through all this hassle to get a baby someone else had by accident?" My anger was put in some perspective when I discovered that the friends who were writing our recommendations for the agency were also indignant, on our behalf, that we should be subjected to such impositions in order to have a child. (We are obviously so well qualified to be parents!) Their vicarious anger made me much more comfortable with my anger.

After acceptance by the agency comes waiting for a child. One may prepare a nursery to assure oneself that a baby is really coming. (An acceptance letter is not as tangible as a pregnancy.) Or one may make no preparations, avoiding raising hopes against the fear that something will go wrong and there will be no baby.

Finally, the agency calls to say, "We have a baby for you to consider." Joy! But joy is followed by a complicated adjustment period. A psychological about-face is required from grieving the loss of the "assumption child" to attaching to an actual baby. Any unresolved feelings about rearing a child not of one's own flesh now surface.

Also startling are the feelings (often shared by biological parents) of discomfort with a newborn or of lack of affection for the baby, of jealousy at the time being spent by a spouse with the baby, or by homemakers of missing the satisfaction and familiarity of former employment. The emotional process of absorbing a child into a family takes time, especially when the nine-month preparatory period of pregnancy is missing. Mixed feelings are a normal, if disconcerting, part of that adjustment.

Grandparents may experience some mixed feelings also. They too miss the preparation time which a pregnancy provides. A grandmother may regret her daughter or daughter-in-law's never experiencing a pregnancy—an important event in the grandmother's life and a part of her female identity which she had looked forward to sharing with her daughter. The child will not have grandpa's eyes. He or she may not look like the parents or grandparents when baby pictures from the family album are compared across generations.

Grandparents may go through their own grieving process as they adjust to the idea of their children adopting. Initially, they may not brag to peers or show off baby pictures. They may be especially reticent if the baby is not matched racially to the family or is visibly handicapped. A double shift in assumptions is being required of them. Also, they may fear a less-than-enthusiastic reaction from friends. The length of time grandparents require to work out their disappointment will depend, in part, on their feelings about children born out of wedlock (assuming that is the case), adoption, the particular characteristics of the infant, and the extent to which the infertile couple has kept them informed throughout the couple's adjustment period.

Most grandparents come to love their adopted grandchildren. Babies can be very engaging. As grandparents feed the child, take pictures, and pick out gifts or clothes, these actions make the situation real for them. Usually, the more involved grandparents can be, the quicker the baby becomes "theirs."

Grandparents may even grow. Julia told me that her father used to hold some racial prejudices. But when Julia and Ben adopted their daughter, from Korea, her father was so delighted for them to have a long-awaited child that he set aside his prejudices. "He really grew to welcome his grandchild into his heart. I was so proud of him."

What has been said here about adopting assumes that the child is an infant. Adopting an older child (age one year and up) and long-term foster care are other options. Such a child comes not only with hereditary factors set, but also with a self-image, and values partially developed. Often this self-image, and accompanying behavior, is not good; older children are usually available because they have been removed from neglectful or abusive homes. Family therapist Virginia Satir describes the family as a mobile: "If a new member is added, the mobile will swing wildly until everyone finds his new place and settles down." This is an apt description of the adjustment required of both parents and child in such adoptions.

This option should be considered only if the couple is prepared to do emotional repair work, can find totally acceptable a child who will always evidence the influence of another family environment, has the support of friends and family, and has access to professional counseling for themselves and the child. Older children are available for adoption more readily than infants.

For the couple willing to consider an especially needy child or a sibling group (children from the same family to be adopted together), several organizations can provide national referrals and assistance. The following sources can be contacted:

The Adoption Center of Delaware Valley
1218 Chestnut Street
Philadelphia, Pennsylvania   19107
(215) 925-0200

CAP Book
700 Exchange Street
Rochester, New York   14608
(716) 232-5110

North American Council on Adoptable Children
1346 Connecticut Avenue N.W.
Washington, D.C.   20036
(202) 466-7570

Artificial Insemination and Surrogate Mothers

A couple in which one spouse is exclusively responsible for the medical infertility has another option. The fertile partner may be the biological parent of a child—the woman by artificial insemination, the man by a surrogate mother.

Artificial insemination is usually accomplished with semen from an anonymous donor, arranged for by the doctor. (Many doctors will not perform this procedure unless the donor is anonymous.) Semen is commonly obtained from college or medical students. Fertility specialists often are affiliated with teaching hospitals, and so can arrange for such a donor to be "on call" on the day a woman should ovulate and two days later. Success rates are estimated at 70% in six ovulatory cycles—a similar fertility rate to that of healthy fertile couples trying to conceive.[3]

Semen may also be obtained, frozen, from a sperm bank. This source is more expensive, but may make available a donor with physical characteristics better matched to the husband's. If a doctor is obtaining fresh semen, the couple should ask about the doctor's record keeping. Some doctors keep records of donors. Others do not, often to guarantee confidentiality or prevent legal questions concerning paternity in states where the consequences of artificial insemination are not specifically spelled out by law. The couple should learn everything possible about the donor, short of his name. Medical history will alert them to possible problems. Family history will allow them to share some day with the child this part of his or her identity, should they choose to tell the child of the circumstances surrounding conception.

Artificial insemination requires an emotional adjustment, especially for the man. The baby is biologically hers but not his, as opposed to adoption where both spouses are on equal footing. The risk is that for a man and woman who have not come to terms with his infertility, the baby may become emotionally hers but not his. Precisely because the couple need not explain to anyone the circumstances of the child's conception, they may never find opportunity to talk out unsettled feelings. The secret of the man's "defect" may burden them for life. A couple looking for help will find none in the literature. Many books are available to counsel adopting parents and their children, but I know of none for couples choosing artificial insemination. If I were choosing this option, I would ask my doctor to put me in touch with several other couples who had given birth to children this way in order to have a chance to talk. Fenton and Lifchez estimate that six to ten thousand babies are born each year using artificial insemination by anonymous donor.[4]

For a couple in which the woman is medically infertile, use of a surrogate mother is an option. The surrogate mother is artificially inseminated with the husband's sperm and carries and bears a child which she releases legally to the couple for adoption. Surrogate mothering was more common in ancient times. "Now Sarai, Abram's wife, bore him no children. She had an Egyptian maid whose name was Hagar; and Sarai said to Abram, 'Behold now, the Lord has prevented me from bearing children; go in to my maid; it may be that I shall obtain children by her'" (Gen. 16:1-2). In ancient times, the morality of the procedure was not at issue and, for purposes of law, all children belonged to the father, and the surrogate mother had no claims. But it was not an option openly discussed in contemporary Western society until the last several years.

If one is considering this option, and has available an acceptable surrogate who is willing to withstand the possible disapprobation of her family, friends, physician, and community, then one must consider, preferably with the surrogate, her husband (in many states a husband is legally the father of any child born in wedlock) and a lawyer some "what ifs". For example, what if the surrogate decides to keep the baby? (In many states a biological mother cannot release a baby until several days after birth.) What are the paternity responsibilities if the surrogate chooses to keep the baby? What if the baby miscarries or is born handicapped? Who pays which expenses?

Use of a surrogate mother raises other difficulties. The procedure may be very expensive, with fees up to $10,000, since the surrogate makes a considerable investment of time, loss of employment, and risk to her health in carrying and bearing a baby. Surrogate mothering is not well-accepted in our society, and the community may view the procedure as immoral. A number of legal problems are raised as well. The rights and obligations of the father are not delineated by the laws of most states. The payment of fees in excess of out-of-pocket medical expenses may be viewed as "baby-selling," which could render any contractual arrangements with the surrogate unenforceable or which in some states might arguably violate criminal laws. Knowledgeable legal counsel is a must, but may be hard to find.

For couples who do not have a surrogate available, few agencies exist to offer assistance. I know of three:

Surrogate Parenting Association—Louisville, Kentucky
Surrogate Parenting, Inc.—North Hollywood, California
Surrogate Mothering, Ltd.—Philadelphia, Pennsylvania

These organizations have established procedures intended to protect both the surrogate and the parent-to-be, and fees intended to compensate the surrogate and pay medical expenses.

The process of deciding which option to exercise is individual to each infertile couple. Some know immediately that if they cannot bear children, they will adopt. Other couples are not so sure and may take months or years to think about the possibilities before choosing their option.

6

Factors
that Influence
Healing

Infertility injures emotional health. The healing process is charted in Chapter 2. Why do some people traverse these emotional stages more quickly, and with less disruption to their daily living patterns and relationships, than others? If we compare an emotional injury to a physical injury, the recovery processes offer some enlightening parallels. The resemblances may clarify points in the emotional healing process where family and friends have opportunity to help.

What factors promote rapid healing with minimum scarring? One determinant of the prognosis for physical healing is the amount of time which passes before an injury is attended. If a person refuses to acknowledge a wound, it does not usually heal itself, but rather is aggravated by the lack of care. Like a neglected physical ailment, unattended emotions, resultant from infertility, may fester and even erupt. An advertising account manager was being interviewed by a new higher-up at the company. What were her goals for the next year, the boss asked by way of learning the aspirations of those he would supervise. "I want to get pregnant," she blurted out and burst into tears. Her concern for possible infertility, which she had been "trying not to worry about," intruded into her professional life.

I had not realized that my concern about possible infertility was affecting my job performance until a coworker asked if I had had a checkup lately. "You seem so lethargic," she said, "I just wondered if you might be anemic or depressed about something." As she spoke, I knew the cause and shared my fears with her. Her understanding response included quiet comments to alert me on days I was functioning poorly. Her support helped me minimize the interference to my work situation caused by infertility.

Having recognized the emotional stresses caused by infertility, the person can focus on containing the effects, lessening the disruption of other areas of functioning. One factor in healing, then, is to overcome initial denial, not only of the medical problem (see Chapter 2), but also of the emotional havoc which accompanies infertility.

A second factor is the extent of the injury. Some severe physical injuries cannot be treated all at once. The body must first be allowed time to stabilize from the shock of the injury before reconstruction can proceed. So with infertility. As the medical testing progresses toward confirmation of medical infertility, the emotional defenses must be broken down toward acceptance of this diagnosis. First denial, then defiance, and finally bargaining fail as protection and are abandoned. Even if a conclusive diagnosis of infertility is reached early in the medical testing, the person must still struggle through layers of defenses. The loss of the "assumption child" is a serious injury to the sense of self that cannot be absorbed all at once. The person maintains defenses for a while, as buffering against the full impact of the reality of infertility. "It just does not seem real," Tom said after learning he was medically infertile. "Nothing tangible in my life has changed, and yet everything has." With time, the initial numbness would dissolve, and the implications sink in. But until the defenses have been completely discarded, it is too early to proceed with the rehabilitative period of choosing an option.

A third factor is time. The person must allow enough time for healing to be complete. Emotional healing cannot be rushed any more than physical healing. How much time? Research with persons recently bereaved indicates that while the "man on the street" thought recovery should take a month or so, in fact, recovery takes about two years.[1] As one widow told me, "a year for tears and a year for anniversaries." With infertility, perhaps, it is a year for the medical testing that confirms infertility, and the emotional process of accepting these results, and a year for working out the option chosen afterwards—to apply for adoption or to find opportunities for enjoying the children of others.

Some people try to circumvent the healing process by declaring themselves recovered. This is a variation of denial. Just as physical infertility is hard to accept, so is the length and imposition of the period of emotional recovery that follows. Carol tried to rush healing. She is a competent professional woman. Sure, she was angry and upset, she would say flatly, but she "really didn't have time to be depressed." She could cope. Three months after she suspected infertility, it was confirmed medically. Two months later she declared herself to be recovered emotionally and stated her intentions to adopt. But, somehow, she did not get around to it. She was "so busy." Five months later she came apart. She got into her car and drove for six hours before she realized that she had no idea where she was going. She did not even have her purse with her; dollar bills in her pocket bought the gas to get her home. The next day she had trouble remembering the incident. Frightened and confused, she sought counseling. Having destroyed her image of herself as coping, by running away in a daze, she was finally able to stop her business and let her depression and pain catch up to her. Three months and many tears later, her sense of direction had returned. She was able to follow through with her plans to apply for adoption.

Carol was trying to bypass the painful aspects of healing by skipping to the concluding phase—that of choosing an acceptable option for her future. She reasoned that she would resolve her problem by acting on that option. But the depression intrinsic in infertility must be accepted and grappled with at a "gut" level as well as pondered at an intellectual level. The intellect can usually process the fact of infertility quickly, but the gut takes much longer. The problem is that this gut-level acceptance must be completed before a selection of an option can be wisely made and successfully commenced. To think we can avoid the gut-level component of healing, or rush it, is to delude ourselves. Emotional healing does not conform to a logical timetable. Healing takes time.

A factor which promotes healing is telling others of one's situation. "Give sorrow words" wrote Shakespeare. "The grief that does not speak knits up the o'erwrought heart and bids it break."[2] "Talking it through" helps clarify one's feelings. Sharing can be hard. It was several months after I knew I was infertile before I mustered the courage to tell my best friend. Even then it took me three false starts in the conversation before I could force the words out of my mouth. Telling myself I was infertile was much easier than telling someone else. The difficulty I experienced in sharing told me that I still harbored denial, that I was less accepting of my infertility than I thought. I was surprised, too, at how apprehensive I was about my friend's reaction. My sense of self was still very vulnerable to the attitudes of others about my "defect."

The reactions of others can open avenues of healing. My friend reacted with sadness and anger on my behalf. Her sentiments affirmed the reality of my injury and my worth in spite of it. Her pain, for me, made my pain more real, but less frightening, because she was willing to risk it with me.

Talking it through helps in identifying which emotions are still painful and which have been overcome or have some source other than the infertility problem. It provides feedback from a friend or counselor by which to gauge the progress of healing.

Research with women recently widowed confirms the need to talk it through repeatedly. Those who had opportunity to talk about their loss and the changes in their life expectations suffered fewer physical ills than those who lacked opportunity to talk.[3] (Incidents of physical illness increase with emotional stress.) Friends and family can make an enormous impact at this point. By being available, by asking about the progress of the testing and of the person's feelings, and by listening patiently, friends aid the person in talking through infertility.

The value of this talking-through process does not seem so strange if we consider how people assimilate good news. We eagerly share the happy events of life. Writing birth announcements and phoning the details to relatives somehow make the monumental change of becoming a parent seem more real. The joy of others helps the event sink in. In the same way sharing the sad news of infertility, and feeling the pain of others on one's behalf, helps one assimilate infertility.

Issues of infertility that are not worked through do not go away. Julie has known her infertility for many years. Her children, adopted as infants, are in grade school. When I asked if I might interview her for this book, she hesitated, "I don't think I can remember much. That was so long ago." But she agreed. Toward the end of the interview she confided, "Truth is, I was scared. I was not sure what we might dredge up. The old memories really flooded back, but I am glad we talked. I told you things I've never told anyone. Maybe I laid some ghosts to rest." Issues and feelings that are not resolved by talking them through during the years of recovery from infertility may be recalled and resolved later by thinking them through out loud in the company of a trusted other.

A person who has a healthy positive self-image and serviceable coping patterns can be expected to recover from infertility more quickly than a person who does not, just as a person who is in good physical condition usually recovers from a physical injury faster than a person who is not. Going into infertility with many sources of self-worth lets one sustain the drain of infertility. If a person is sure she or he is of value beforehand, then that person will still be of value, even after discovery of a "defect" like infertility. People who have few claims for self-worth as an adult, beyond becoming a parent, may wonder after infertility strikes if life is worth living. Positive self-esteem helps fend off suicidal thoughts during the depression period of healing. Knowing that one is valued by others and for other qualities motivates one to heal and get beyond infertility.

Self-worth also affects the relationship to one's spouse. If I am of value in spite of my infertility, then I continue to be worthy of the love of my spouse despite my flaw. At some point, most medically infertile persons wonder whether their spouse would be better off alone—at least then the other could remarry and bear children. A person with a shaky self-image is more likely to act on this. Feeling unworthy, the medically infertile individual may push the spouse away, refusing the support that the other may be trying to give. "How could anyone want to live with someone as depressed and as depressing to be around as I am? We don't even enjoy sex any more. I am sure he would rather be with someone more fun—and more fertile."

Consistent reassurance of the spouse will help. A person with a positive sense of esteem is more likely to have married a mate with good emotional resources. That spouse will be less depleted by infertility and is likely to be more supportive. Health is a self-feeding cycle.

As with spouse, so with friends. Good friends who listen and help one think through infertility without rushing to "make it all better" aid healing. A person who enters infertility with a healthy sense of self is more likely to have such friends. He or she will also be more willing to risk allowing friends to know and so permit them to support.

For some, belief in God acts as an anchor for self-esteem. If one believes that God's love is unconditional, religious belief can confirm the value of the person in spite of infertility. This spiritual component can be an added source of self-esteem.

Good health includes regular habits of exercise. For emotional health this means well-developed coping patterns for stress. One of the coping mechanisms of people who are most successful in business is that before tackling a problem they imagine the worst possible result. They confront it, examine it, and decide if and how they would survive it.[4] In the context of infertility, the worst might be that one would be childless for life, or have to adopt in order to parent, or may have a marriage relationship stressed to the breaking point.

Having looked at the worst, one should next decide what part of it cannot be avoided. Here the medical examination serves. It is essential to be able to accept the results of medical testing—after getting a second opinion, just to be sure. Having laid aside what one cannot change and having grieved the loss, one tries to act on the things that can be modified. Choosing manageable chunks helps. Today I will call one doctor, or talk to my spouse about the possibility of adoption, or go to work and back without crying. One regains some feeling of control over an overwhelming problem when one can accomplish the task earmarked for the day.

The habit of seeking and accepting others' help is useful, whether from friends or from counselors. Emotional wounds may require professional counseling just as physical wounds may require expert treatment. Or outside help may be sufficiently provided by friends. If one's former coping patterns include sharing with a friend, then when infertility strikes, one already has a trusted confidante with whom to think through this problem.

As a person who is recuperating from a physical injury is vulnerable to complications, so a person adjusting to infertility is vulnerable to other emotional assaults. Loss of a job, divorce, a serious physical illness or the death of a loved one, while always hard to deal with, may at this time be beyond the capacity of the person to bear. Coping patterns that could have withstood one emotional onslaught can collapse under the overload of two. Infertility hurts. Being hurt twice in close succession may result in a person's withdrawing from all relationships. Unwilling to risk overwhelming hurt a third time, the person becomes emotionally numb or flees reality. Such a person may become a recluse or suffer a nervous breakdown.

The completion of healing in infertility often comes as the person chooses and learns to live with an alternative to giving birth to a child. Different options meet the needs of different people and are discussed in Chapter 5. I chose adoption. I have the two children I always wanted, spaced apart as I wanted, a little later in life than I had planned. They have dulled the pain of infertility to a quiet, occasional sadness that I missed the experience of pregnancy and the chance to see my husband's math aptitude perpetuated in his child.

If I had it to do again, I would want to get pregnant. But if I were offered that option now, I would not. I have the family I always desired. Choosing a livable option does not eliminate the emotional scars of infertility, but it may complete the healing process. I no longer hurt.

A person suffering through infertility often feels alone. "How can anyone possibly understand the agony I am going through, unless they have been there?" In fact, infertility is but one of many grieving processes. A grieving process is the emotional adjustment to a loss—for example, the loss of a job of long standing, of one's home to fire, or of a loved one, especially a child—or divorce, which is the loss of a marriage relationship. Any such loss forces the person into the stages discussed in Chapter 2. Take divorce, for example. Denial—"This can't be happening to us." Anger—"How could he do this to me? I have put up with so much." Or guilt—"I wonder if I'm as bitchy as he says." Bargaining—"Maybe if I don't push him to spend time with the kids, he'll come home nights." "Maybe if I make those kitchen cabinets she wants, she will realize how much she needs me around the house." The despair hits when the person realizes that nothing one person alone can do will save the marriage. Her identity as wife and often her economic security may be lost; his, as husband, provider, or father. The loss is not identical to that of infertility, but the adjustment process is parallel.

The first time through an experience is scary. One does not know what to expect or how bad the worst might be. The first day on a job or the first date, the first hospitalization or the first time out of a job—all are causes for butterflies in the stomach. The second time is not necessarily easy, but at least one knows what to expect and how to cope. The panic is less; one can prepare mentally. The second time through a grieving process can be more manageable and less disruptive to daily functioning, assuming that one has healed from the first. One knows what one must go through and that one will survive. Using this knowledge can take the panic out of infertility.

If one has been through a disappointment or loss before the infertility experience, the similarities can be found. "This depression is like the one I felt when my sister died." Suffering through a depression is less frightening if one knows from experience that eventually it will pass.

If one has not been through a grieving process before, one should seek out friends who have been through a parallel experience and listen to their story. The experience will serve the next time life throws a curve. Friends that are helpful this time can be sought out the next time.

Having been through the grieving process of infertility, a person may be better able to help others in the same or similar circumstances. The memory of one's own pain may prompt one to find better choice of words to help or to understand that one cannot fix another's pain, but can help by being available to listen. I had this experience recently with a friend going through a divorce. I found satisfaction in pulling something useful out of my otherwise useless experience of infertility. That I could help confirmed the validity of my understanding of my own healing process.

Finally, for family and friends, the parallels between infertility and other grieving processes open the way for you to help. You probably have not experienced infertility. But you have, most likely, been through some form of loss. That experience in your own background can be most useful to your understanding and finding words of comfort for the infertile person. Remember the depth of your own pain and what kinds of responses and assurances helped. Use these as guidelines with your infertile friend. Share your experience of loss, if that seems appropriate. You *can* help. The infertile person need not traverse the healing process alone.

7

A Faith
on
God's Terms

Faith in the steadfast love of an all-powerful God shapes one's perception of an infertility experience. Faith does not offer an exemption from the onslaught of painful emotions, but it does provide a framework within which to process these emotions. For me four beliefs concerning the nature of God underlie this framework.

Assumptions about God

First, God is ever-present. I may feel isolated from God by the pain and stigma of infertility; I may cry with the psalmist, "My God, my God, why have you abandoned me?" (Ps. 22:1 TEV), but infertility is not an indication of abandonment by God. The psalmist reassures, "The one you [God] love you will not abandon . . ." (Ps. 16:10 TEV). Confidence in God's constancy mitigates the sense of isolation inherent in infertility. Faith permits me to say, "I am always aware of the Lord's presence" (Ps. 16:8 TEV).

Second, I believe that God loves me. Infertility does not indicate a breach in God's love. Infertility can cause a person to feel unlovely, draining him or her of joy and laughter, leaving sadness and bitterness—attributes not easily loved. Yet nothing in my reaction to infertility can deter God from loving me. Paul assures "that nothing can separate us from the love of God" (Rom. 8:38). Confidence in God's love lessens that sense of unloveliness.

Third, God values me. Infertility is not a defect which depreciates my importance before God. One's sense of self-worth may be threatened or diminished by infertility, but an infertile person is still capable of a relationship with God— of praise and of prayer. When the psalmist says of human beings, "Yet you made him inferior only to yourself: you crowned him with glory and honor" (Ps. 8:5 TEV), no qualifier concerning fertility is mentioned. Awareness of God's evaluation helps bolster a sense of self-worth.

Fourth, God calls me to further his work. Infertility does not exempt me from the call to serve others. God does not accept defects or frailties as excuses. He has fully considered the limitations of his believers before issuing his call to them to be his ambassadors. Witness Moses, who cited no less than four limitations which he argued disqualified him from accepting God's assignment to journey to Egypt and speak to Pharaoh (Exod. 3:11, 3:13, 4:1, 4:10). God answers each limitation and then orders, "Now, go! I will help you . . ." (Exod. 4:12 TEV). Since my infertility does not rob me of the capacity to minister to my neighbor, it does not excuse me from my obligation to act in God's service to my neighbor.

The Challenge of Unmerited Suffering

But if God loves me, why did he permit my infertility in the first place? Presumably God could prevent infertility; presumably God cares that I suffer. Why, then, does he permit suffering? The four theories of suffering which follow are based on my experience and that of the infertile Christians I interviewed.

1. Perhaps God inflicts infertility as punishment for sin. "If you listen to these commands and obey them faithfully, . . . none of you nor any of your cattle will be sterile" (Deut. 7:12-14 TEV). But if one worships false gods, one will "have no children, because you have turned away from me" (Hosea 4:10 TEV). The Israelites believed God, rather than chance, to be the force determining the fertility and well-being of their population. If infertility occurred, Israel must have sinned. Righteous individuals were understood to suffer barrenness along with the less virtuous, because responsibility for sin was seen as corporate. God had covenanted with the people of Israel as a single entity, and thus God judged the people corporately.

But God's justice has correctional as well as retributive aspects. God punishes Israel out of love as well as out of anger, hoping to impress upon the Hebrews the gravity of their sins and the urgency of their need to repent. "Have I any pleasure in the death [or infertility] of the wicked, says the Lord God, and not rather that he should turn from his way and live?" (Ezek. 18:23). A modern parallel might be a parent spanking a child for running out into the street without first checking for traffic. The parent intends the spanking not only to convey anger, but also, and more importantly, to impress the child with the seriousness of breaching the parent's rules and the intensity of the parent's desire that the rules be followed. Concern for the health and safety of the child motivates the parent.

Surely we do suffer from our sin and the sin of others. God forgives the sin, but does not necessarily negate the effect of sinful acts. One criminal crucified beside Jesus asks for, and receives, forgiveness for his sins (Luke 23:40-43). He is not, however, rescued from the cross, which is a consequence of his sinful act, nor are arrangements made to compensate the victims of his crimes for their suffering and loss at his hands. But infertility is usually not the direct physical consequence of a particular sinful act. A smoker may knowingly risk emphysema or a drunk driver cause an unnecessary auto fatality, but most infertile persons have not committed any offense for which infertility is the byproduct.

Is infertility, then, a form of retribution for sin, whether of an individual or a people? In the Old Testament responsibility for sin is corporate; God relates to and covenants with all the people of Israel as a single entity. In the New Testament sin is an individual responsibility; through Jesus and the Holy Spirit, God relates to and covenants with individuals. This does not mean that one person's wrongdoings do not affect others, but rather that each person has direct access to God and is ultimately responsible for that relationship to God. "What do you mean repeating this proverb concerning the land of Israel, 'The fathers have eaten sour grapes and the children's teeth are set on edge'? As I live, says the Lord God, this proverb shall no more be used by you in Israel. Behold, all souls are mine; the soul of the father as well as the soul of the son is mine; the soul that sins shall die" (Ezek. 18:2-4). Infertility is not, therefore, retribution for the sins "of the fathers."

Is infertility retribution for one's own sins? Jesus specifically refutes the contention that suffering is proof of sin (Luke 13:1-5). Furthermore, Christ's crucifixion satisfies for all time God's requirement that sin be punished. For a Christian who knows forgiveness through Christ, infertility cannot be accounted for as retribution for sin. "There is no condemnation now for those who live in union with Christ Jesus" (Rom. 8:1 TEV). While ancient Hebrews could consider that God ordained their suffering as evidence of and retribution for their sins, Christians must seek an explanation elsewhere.

Although infertility is not retribution for sin, might it not still be used by God to demand attendance to his call for repentance—like the parent spanking the child to impress upon that child the necessity of checking for traffic before crossing the street? If the infertility is temporary and God, through the Holy Spirit sends an explanation, then perhaps so. God blinded Paul for three days in order to arrest his attention. God immediately stated his message and soon there after lifted Paul's blindness (Acts 9:3-19).

Permanent infertility cannot be explained in this way. Although the infertile person turns to God, seeking instruction, the infertility remains. God has this person's attention; why would he continue to allow suffering which is now pointless?

Infertility for the person who does not respond by turning to God makes no sense either. If God fails to reach a person with one form of communication, he tries another. In the Old Testament, when the message of one prophet does not succeed in returning Israel's focus toward him, God sends another prophet to try a different approach. A loving parent does not continue to spank a child if the spanking is not getting the point across. To do so would be retributive rather than correctional.

Infertility is an ambiguous mode of communication in any event, being open to a range of interpretations. Arresting a person's attention with suffering which the person does not understand makes no more sense than spanking a child who does not understand what action provoked the spanking. Thus unless infertility is very temporary, and explained specifically by God, it is probably not a call from God for repentance.

2. A second possible explanation is that God uses infertility, and other suffering, to prepare Christians for the rigors of service as his ambassadors to others. From this viewpoint, infertility is not an indication of sin, but rather a tool employed by God to prepare his people for some future task— perhaps to steel their trust in and resolve to obey God's commands, or perhaps to increase their compassion for and responsiveness to the sufferings of others. God is like a coach pushing an athlete through exhausting training to prepare that athlete for an upcoming contest. As the athlete's skills increase through the training program, his or her confidence in the coach also increases. This theory of suffering as training shares with the theory of retribution the belief that suffering is God's way of sending a message to the sufferer. It is pur-

poseful. The difference is that the message for those who view suffering as training is one of opportunity rather than of judgment.

The assumption behind this viewpoint is that God, in his fatherly love, arranges all circumstances to work toward the benefit and growth of his children. This is one possible understanding of Paul's statement: "For we know that in everything God works for good with those who love him, who are called according to his purpose" (Rom. 8:28). Not all circumstances will be pleasant, but each will offer the Christian opportunity to grow in relationship to God. Thus, we are not to be preoccupied about physical needs, what we will eat or drink or wear (Luke 12:22-31). Rather, the Christian is to ask God and he will provide what he deems necessary and useful. "How much more will your Father who is in heaven give good things to those who ask him!" (Matt. 7:11).

A belief that God governs all circumstances to promote the Christian's spiritual well-being provides assurance that, regardless of the power or limitations of medical science, God will determine one's future fertility or infertility. While the Christian may be powerless to alter fertility, God is not so limited. The knowledge that while God may use infertility to stretch the Christian's faith, he "will not allow you to be tested beyond your power to remain firm" (1 Cor. 10:13) frees the believer from the fear of inability to cope with the pain and trauma of infertility. Trusting in God's goodness, the Christian seeks the lesson God offers through infertility and watches for situations in which new wisdom may be used to aid others in Christ's name.

The theory of infertility as a training exercise contains two difficulties. First, infertility is purposeful only as it produces the result God desires. Either the experience of infertility effects the desired result or it fails to do so. For God to continue infertility as a permanent training exercise can achieve only suffering, which makes at least permanent infertility an experience of judgment rather than opportunity.

Second, the commitment of a Christian to God's service,

like the commitment of an athlete to a sport, is an ongoing process. The person who makes an initial commitment to serve God neither forfeits free will nor absolves him or herself of the responsibility to participate actively in the training program. The Christian always retains options. If infertility is training, the Christian should be able to abandon the training program and have fertility restored. But this is not the case; one cannot decide that the pain is not worth the gain, and quit.

3. A third possible understanding of infertility is as a message from God to rethink one's life plans. The message might be a suggestion to forego the ties and responsibilities of children to be free for some other service, or, perhaps God wishes one to adopt. This view assumes that circumstances reflect God's will and that the blocking of an option is a sign from God pointing toward a different opportunity.

While God may use circumstances to reflect his will, God's foremost method of communication with believers is the Holy Spirit. The Christian must seek the counsel of the Holy Spirit, both in prayer and in discussion with other Christians, before attributing a particular message from God to infertility.

4. A fourth possible understanding of infertility is that such suffering is not a direct message from God. Unlike the three preceding possibilities, this theory does not assume that suffering is purposeful. At the least, God's reasons for allowing suffering are acknowledged to be beyond human understanding. This response to unmerited suffering is suggested several places in the Bible. For example, when Job rails at God, protesting his unprovoked suffering, God answers, "Who are you to question my wisdom with your ignorant, empty words?" (Job 38:2 TEV). Having experienced God's power, Job is humbled. He no longer demands that God limit his actions to those which Job can comprehend.

Habakkuk has a similar experience, when he angrily questions God's timing and methods of punishment for Judah. God responds to Habakkuk's questions not with an explanation for his actions, but rather with a display of his power

and a challenge to Habakkuk to believe in God's love despite
the apparent unreasonableness of his actions. Like Job, Habakkuk realizes that his relationship with God is not based on
favorable circumstances—health or prosperity—but rather on
the experience of God's prerogative to act in his own time and
beyond human understanding. Habakkuk experiences God's
faithfulness and caring, enabling him to meet imminent suffering with inner calm (Hab. 3:17-18).

The New Testament offers a third example of God's responding to a request for the removal of suffering with a call
for faith. When Paul asks God for the cessation of a chronic
physical ailment, God responds, "My grace is all you need"
(2 Cor. 12:9). Perhaps the same answer applies to infertility.

The sufferer must then decide whether God's responsive
demand is acceptable. At this juncture some infertile persons
turn their backs on God. Others accept God's prerogative to
allow things that humans are not capable of understanding,
even infertility. It is not easy to continue to believe in a God
who demands acceptance of infertility almost without explanation. It is not easy to harmonize God's loving nature with
the existence of suffering. Just as the process of coping with
infertility requires a redefinition of one's self-image, which
includes infertility, so the process of coping with this understanding of God's response requires a rethinking of one's
relationship with God.

Reconstructing a Relationship with God

As set forth in Chapter 2, the process of redefining one's
self-image includes three stages: (1) attempts to deny, avoid
responsibility for, or banish the threat of a destruction of
one's assumptions; (2) recognition and acceptance of the loss
of one's assumptions; (3) formation and integration of new
assumptions. This process applies to changes in one's relationship to God as well as to changes in one's assumptions
concerning infertility.

In the first stage the person acts to prevent infertility from affecting the relationship with God. One denies that infertility has the potential to affect one's belief. For example, "If I learn I am permanently infertile, that will not alter my faith," June said. One attempts to understand the ramifications of possible infertility on the relationship with God, and when no understandable reason emerges, one churns with anger at the inability to even comprehend, much less control, fate. "God, how dare you threaten my faith with infertility? You healed others when they asked, thereby confirming your power. Why do you leave me with so many doubts?" I prayed such "prayers" often during my adjustment to infertility. Then one attempts to bargain with God for a removal of the threat to one's faith. Just as Hannah begged for a son, so the Christian may beg for security of faith, promising dedication to God's service and vowing not to request any further favors related to fertility.

In the second stage one recognizes that just as denial, anger, or bargaining did not avert infertility, so also they did not dissuade God from allowing the challenges to faith that accompany infertility. While God displayed his kindness to Rachel and to Samson's mother by answering their prayers for children, he displays no such inclination toward the Christian who remains infertile. (The stories and prayers of ancient Hebrew women who remained childless are not remembered in the Bible, perhaps because they do not so clearly confirm the power of God.) Faith is now challenged, rather than confirmed, by circumstances. One weeps for the loss of the comfort and security which faith formerly supplied. Before moving on to the third stage, one must set aside those assumptions about faith which infertility has invalidated.

In the third stage one establishes a renewed relationship to God, founded more on the experience of grace and less on the evidence of events than former faith. Just as the relinquishing of former faith was a process consisting of several phases rather than a single event, so the renewal of a relationship is also a process. Habakkuk's experience offers an example of such a process. Habakkuk suffered the loss of former assumptions concerning God's future acts in response to Judah's sin and suffering. Having presented his confusion and distress to God and having heard God's declaration of power and call to faithfulness, Habakkuk responded in a manner noteworthy to infertile Christians who wish to rebuild their relationship with God. He listened: "O Lord, I have heard of what you have done, and I am filled with awe" (Hab. 3:2 TEV). He recognized that God is God: "I tremble" (Hab. 3:16 TEV). He affirmed God's capacity to do what is good and appropriate in God's own time: "I will quietly wait for the time to come . . ." (Hab. 3:16 TEV). Finally, he declared his faith and the hope it brought even in painful, difficult situations: "Though the fig tree do not blossom, nor fruit be on the vines, . . . yet I will rejoice in the Lord, I will joy in the God of my salvation" (Hab. 3:17-18). Having met God in the midst of suffering, Habakkuk then offered his experience of comfort to his people who suffered in the same situation. His experience of God's grace enabled Habakkuk to assist others.

While infertility may not be imposed by God in order to induce growth, the grappling with infertility and with God's intentions may produce growth in a Christian. This is the alternative understanding of Paul's declaration: "We know that in everything God works for good with those who love him according to his purpose" (Rom. 8:28). This process of resolving the doubts and anger arising out of infertility and of wrestling and realigning with God requires tenacity bordering on stubbornness. God's challenge to the Christian to be a part of his work for good even in suffering, gives the Christian a focus amid the chaos of emotions that accompany infertility. God's promise of involvement in this struggle, gives the Christian hope. This process takes time, and it is during this time that other Christians have the opportunity to be of particular support.

The Role of the Christian Community

It is the privilege of Christians to act as God's emissaries to infertile individuals. "So we are ambassadors for Christ, God making his appeal through us" (2 Cor. 5:20). Because the infertile person experiences uncertainty about the nature, intent or even existence of God, the person is particularly sensitive to the kindness or callousness of Christians. Of the twelve couples I interviewed, two had been drawn into the fellowship of a church because of comfort and support offered them. Two others who were already Christian credited Christian friends with helping them weather the trauma of their infertility. But one, who had once been Christian, abandoned her faith because of insensitive remarks from other Christians.

The intervention of fellow believers strongly influenced these infertile persons' understanding of their relationship with God, and God's grace. The Christian's opportunity is to interact with the infertile person in such a way that the person experiences the nature and grace of God through the compassionate behavior of the Christian. The list of dos and don'ts in Chapter 2 can be understood in the context of the four beliefs concerning the nature of God outlined at the beginning of this chapter.

God is ever-present, so the Christian is called to be present—to let the infertile couple know that the Christian is aware of, or suspects, the infertility and is available to help in whatever way possible.

God loves, so the Christian cares enough to listen—to shoulder part of the pain of infertility, accepting the further agony of knowing that he or she can offer nothing that will eliminate the pain.

God values, so the Christian confirms the person's self-worth, gently but persistently seeking that person's company—both for what can be offered that person and for what that person can offer in return.

God calls, so the Christian encourages and challenges the

infertile person to sustain and strengthen relationships with others, especially the spouse, and to give service to others.

Just as the list of dos fits into the context of faith, so also the list of don'ts can be considered in that same context. While the Christian is to be aware of the extent of the problem of infertility, to be sensitive to signs of infertility in others, to take the initiative in relating to infertile persons, and to offer to share the pain, it is the choice of the infertile person to accept or reject another's offer of caring. God calls his children to reach out to each other; he does not require the outreach to succeed. The credit for the success or the blame for the failure of outreach and caring lies with the infertile person and with God. Awareness of this allows a believer to back off gracefully when the person is not ready or chooses not to accept the offer of caring. And by backing off gracefully, the Christian leaves the option open for the infertile person to request support at some later time.

While the Christian is called to share the pain of the infertile person, "to weep with those who weep" (Rom. 12:15), the Christian is not responsible for explaining suffering or curing it.

The Christian is called to value the infertile person, but not to explain the value of that suffering. This chapter offered four possible explanations for God's allowing infertility. The comments most offensive to infertile Christians I interviewed were those which assumed a theory of suffering different from that of the listener. For example, "Maybe God is trying to tell you something" assumes that suffering is intended to be a direct message, either as training or as guidance toward a different plan for life. Likewise, "You should relax, God will provide what's best" assumes the "suffering as training" theory. (It also pronounces a negative judgment on the sufferer's feelings of anger toward God—anger which is an honest and essential part of the sufferer's progress towards a renewed relationship with God.) Neither comment is helpful to a person who has a different understanding of God's intent. While one might share one's perception of suffering if invited to do so, gratuitous comments are usually unwelcome. The infertile person does not need explanation, but rather someone who will listen and empathize.

Finally, the Christian is called to encourage and challenge the infertile person to relate to and serve others, but not to judge if the infertile person does not immediately respond to this call. The infertile person's energy is depleted, and a pause for rest and reorientation is needed. Even Jesus went off by himself for a 40-day retreat to consider his own identity and role as the Son of God, before beginning his ministry to others (Matt. 4:1-11). Throughout this experience, the infertile person does not need judgment, which depletes self-worth, but grace, which confirms and nurtures the person toward spiritual and emotional health through the love of God as reflected through Christians.

It is risky to open oneself to the pain and doubts of the infertile person, to undertake to support the person empathically. It is risky, too, for the infertile person to accept that support and trust, to lay open the doubts and the suffering. But the isolation which is the alternative is worse. So, let us affirm each other by sharing and responding, trusting in the sufficiency of the grace of God, who loves us.

Notes

Chapter 1

1   Novak, Jones, and Jones, *Novak's Textbook of Gyne-
     cology* (Baltimore: Waverly Press, 1975), p. 625.
2   Novak, Jones, and Jones, *Novak's Textbook of Gyne-
     cology*, p. 625.

Chapter 2

1   Stan and Jan Berenstain, *He Bear, She Bear* (New
     York: Random House, 1974).
2   Mary Harrison, *Infertility* (Boston: Houghton Mif-
     flin, 1977), p. 3.
3   Susan Nixon, "For Want of a Child," *Chicago* 29
     (December 1980, no. 12) :219.
4   *Resolve Newsletter* (Belmont, Mass.: Resolve Inc.),
     June 1980.
5   Harrison, *Infertility*, p. 88.
6   Nixon, "For Want of a Child," p. 215.
7   Thomas Ball, *Gynecologic Surgery & Urology* (St.
     Louis: Mosby, 1963), p. 31.
8   *Resolve Newsletter*, June 1980.

9   Harrison, *Infertility*, p. 87.
10   Harrison, *Infertility*, p. 87.
11   Richard Phillips, "Infertility," *Chicago Tribune*, December 7, 1980, sec. 12, p. 4.

Chapter 3

1   Sherwin Kaufman, *New Hope for the Childless Couple* (New York: Simon & Schuster, 1970), p. 32.
2   David Rosenfeld and Eileen Mitchell, "Treating the Emotional Aspects of Infertility: Counseling Services in an Infertility Clinic," *American Journal of Obstetrics and Gynecology* 135 (1979, no. 177).

Chapter 4

1   Fenton and Lifchez, *The Fertility Handbook* (New York: Clarkson N. Potter, 1980), p. 58.
2   Speroff, Glass, and Case, *Clinical Gynecology, Endocrinology and Infertility* (Baltimore: Williams and Wilkins, 1973).
3   Fenton and Lifchez, *The Fertility Handbook*, p. 82.
4   Fenton and Lifchez, *The Fertility Handbook*, p. 82.
5   Fenton and Lifchez, *The Fertility Handbook*, p. 47.
6   Sherwin Kaufman, *You Can Have a Baby* (Nashville: Thomas Nelson, 1978), p. 35.

Chapter 5

1   Kaufman, *You Can Have a Baby*, p. 117.
2   United States Department of Health, Education, and Welfare figures for 1973, printed in 1975 (most recent available).
3   Fenton and Lifchez, *The Fertility Handbook*, p. 88.
4   Fenton and Lifchez, *The Fertility Handbook*, p. 125.

Chapter 6

1   Glen W. Davidson, "Hospice Care for the Dying,"
      Dying: Facing the Facts (Washington: Hemisphere,
      1979), p. 173.
2   *Macbeth*, IV, 3, 209.
3   Maddison and Walker, "Factors Affecting the Out-
      come of Conjugal Bereavement," *British Journal of
      Psychiatry* 113 (1967): 1057-1067.
4   Erik Larson, "Why Do Some People Outperform
      Others? Psychologist (Charles A. Garfield) Picks
      Out Six Characteristics," *The Wall Street Journal*,
      January 13, 1982, p. 25.

For Further Reading

The following books may be helpful for further reading. Those by fertility specialists offer medical information for laypersons. The autobiographical accounts by infertile individuals usually emphasize the emotional stresses experienced by the author; many include some medical information. The book on miscarriage speaks to both the medical and the emotional aspects of that ordeal. The books on adoption include information about the process of adopting, as well as personal accounts of the joys and trials of adopting and raising adopted children.

Do not be surprised if you feel awkward purchasing a book on infertility, or withdrawing one from a library. I felt obvious—as if I were wearing a sign, "I'm infertile!" That is not information I normally share with strangers. I remember telling a librarian that I needed these books for research I was doing, and then feeling silly afterwards for being still so threatened by this aspect of my identity. Others must feel uncomfortable too; five of the seven books on infertility at my local library were missing, unaccountably, at the time I requested them. A librarian told me that books on this subject are frequently stolen. Many helpful books are available, if one can bring oneself to obtain them.

Decker, Albert and Loebl, Suzanne. *Why Can't We Have a Baby?* New York: The Dial Press, 1978.

A detailed explanation of both normal female and male reproduction, and of causes and treatments of infertility, which includes entertaining historical quotes and sensitive recognition of emotional issues. A good first book.

Dywasuk, Colette Taub. *Adoption—Is It for You?* New York: Harper & Row, 1973.

A guide to decision making, this book also includes a list of adoptive parents' groups.

Fenton, Judith A. and Lifchez, Aaron S. *The Fertility Handbook.* New York: Clarkson N. Potter, Inc., 1980.

Detailed medical information on both female and male causes and treatment. (Most books by fertility specialists who are gynecologists concentrate on female causes and treatment.) Not a good introductory book on infertility because the style is very clinical, but a good reference book if one wants to read in detail about a particular problem or test.

Halverson, Kaye and Hess, Karen. *The Wedded Unmother.* Minneapolis: Augsburg. 1980.

A very personal account of the struggle of a Christian woman to understand her infertility in the context of her faith.

Harrison, Mary. *Infertility, A Guide for the Childless Couple.* Boston: Houghton Mifflin Co., 1977.

Harrison explains her purpose: "to let you know you are not alone, to share with you the painful emotional journey." The book contains both her autobiographical account and some medical information.

Howard, James T. and Schultz, Dodi. *We Want to Have a Baby.* New York: E. P. Dutton, 1979.

A medical explanation of infertility causes and treatment from normal conception, through timing and technique and a normal medical work-up, to fairly rare fertility problems. A short chapter on miscarriage is included. This book aims to help infertile couples understand and use medical services optimally.

Kaufman, Sherwin A. *New Hope for the Childless Couple.* New York: Simon & Schuster, 1970.

A clear description of the medical diagnosis and treatment of infertility (primarily for the female) interspersed with delightful historical anecdotes concerning ancient beliefs about fertility, comments on the development of this area of medical science, and supportive emotional counsel. One of the first books for laypersons.

Kaufman, Sherwin A. *You Can Have a Baby*. New York: Elsevier—Nelson, Inc., 1978.

An update on *New Hope for the Childless Couple* and an excellent first book to read.

Klibanoff, Susan and Elton. *Let's Talk About Adoption*. Boston: Little, Brown & Co., 1973.

A personal description of their experience, plus general information on transracial adoption, birth mothers, the law and the history of adoption.

Livingston, Carole. *Why Was I Adopted?* Secaucus, N.J.: Lyle Stuart Inc., 1978.

Subtitled: "The facts of adoption with love and illustrations." This is a delightful children's picture book that is for adults too. I used it to explain the arrival of our child to the neighborhood children.

Martin, Cynthia D. *Beating the Adoption Game*. San Diego: Oak Tree Publications, 1980.

Menning, Barbara E. *Infertility*. Riverside, CA: NACAC, 1977.

Menning is the founder and former director of Resolve, Inc. In this book she covers all aspects of infertility: the medical, the emotional, and the social.

Pizer, Hank and Palinski, Christine O. *Coping with a Miscarriage*. New York: The Dial Press, 1980.

Palinski is a psychologist who has suffered three miscarriages. Pizer is a physician's assistant and writer. Together they have written a sensitive, succinct book that addresses both the medical and the emotional aspects of miscarriage. An excellent book.

Raymond, Louise. *Adoption and After*. New York: Harper & Row, 1974.

How to prepare oneself for adoption, how to tell a child he or she is adopted, considerations in adopting an older child.

Silber, Sherman J. *How to Get Pregnant*. New York: Scribner, 1980.

Written by a urologist who specializes in infertility, this conversational-style book explores the medical aspects of infertility from basic reproduction to current experimentation in storage of sperm and test-tube babies.

Stangel, John J. *Fertility and Conception*. New York: New American Library, 1979.

A very detailed explanation with over 80 charts and diagrams, from normal reproduction to usual causes and rare treatments of infertility. A good reference book for those who have read less detailed material and want more information.

Van Why, Elizabeth Wharton. *Adoption Bibliography and Multi-Ethnic Sourcebook*. Hartford, Conn.: Open Door Society of Connecticut, 1977.

Lists more than 1250 articles, nonfiction books, personal accounts, and scholarly tomes as well as toys, games, cards, and children's books which reflect African, Asian, Latin American, and Native American heritages. If one wishes a comprehensive list of further readings on adoption, this is it.